The sacred selves
of adolescent girls

The sacred selves of adolescent girls

Hard Stories of Race, Class, and Gender

Edited by

Evelyn L. Parker

WIPF *&* STOCK · Eugene, Oregon

Prayerfully composed for
Iyonna
Airrielle
Benjamin
Xavier
so that you may live in freedom

Wipf and Stock Publishers
199 W 8th Ave, Suite 3
Eugene, OR 97401

The Sacred Selves of Adolescent Girls
Hard Stories of Race, Class, and Gender
By Parker, Evelyn L.
Copyright©2006 Pilgrim Press
ISBN 13: 978-1-60899-390-1
Publication date 1/8/2010
Previously published by Pilgrim Press, 2006

Contents

Introduction

EVELYN L. PARKER

We are born into this world as unsinned, beautiful infants. . . . We are taught to dance and sing. . . . When we die . . . we will dance through the gates of heaven and be at peace with one another.

— Kateri Quoetone and Kim and Pam Ahhaitty,
"Feathers of the Wind: Our Footsteps as Kiowa Young Ladies"

During the 2005 Summer Academy of the Perkins Youth School of Theology (PYST) I was blessed to get to know three young women from the Kiowa Nation of Native America. Kim and Pam are twins and were also that year's Kiowa Princesses. Kateri is their cousin. In the PYST community of twenty-five high school seniors, eight counselors, and four faculty members and their families, these young women gradually became comfortable telling their stories of love and loss, of accomplishments and failures. Upon hearing about the annual Pow Wow hosted by the Taos Pueblo, the PYST Community unanimously agreed to support Kim's wishes to participate in the Pow Wow's Grand March. Pam, Kateri, and Madeline, one of the counselors, went to the event early enough to pay the proper fees and adorn Kim in her beautiful princess dress and jewelry. The rest of the PYST Community arrived to see the pageantry of the event; so beautiful was it that I cried with pride as I witnessed Kim's beauty, grace, and dignity as she danced. This beautiful adolescent female not only represented the Kiowa Nation but our newly formed community.

Kim's dancing embodied her spirituality and reflected all that had together formed her way of knowing and being in the world. Her

1

dancing kinetically captured her spirituality, a spirituality shaped by the merging of Christian beliefs and practices with Kiowa tradition, rituals, and ways of knowing as well as by her experiences of being female, poor, and Native American in the United States. Like the intricate beauty of Kim's beaded breastplate that adorned her dress during the Grand March, her spirituality is complex, multidimensional, and elaborate.

During the last week of the PYST Summer Academy I told Kateri, Pam, and Kim about this book. I asked them to write a brief narrative about how their spirituality was formed in the Kiowa Nation that I might include in the book. Each wrote a draft, and then they combined them, with some editing, into a final version. Almost in ritual fashion, Kateri presented me with "Feathers of the Wind: Our Footsteps as Kiowa Young Ladies." In this essay Kateri, Pam, and Kim expressed the movements of their spiritual formation in the "Kiowa way." Here I share some excerpts from their writing, just as they presented it to me. They spoke of being blessed and baptized by their grandfathers, who were once preachers, and growing up in church, singing Kiowa hymns, and "Haw, Ah-ho Daw-kee, thanking God for what he's done." They described being taught the ways of Kiowa women, "to dance, sign, bead, sew, and cook . . . setting the table . . . the women eat last." They are taught the Kiowa language by their grandparents and instructed to talk only Kiowa to their elders to show them respect. In Kateri's draft she wrote, "If we wanted something passed to us during dinner we would have to ask in Kiowa, a very cultural way of life, I think. I actually think the girls had it harder than the boys or men, but that's just how it is." The closing lines of "Feathers of the Wind" illustrate the multidimensional and elaborate nature of their spirituality.

> When somebody we love dearly dies,
> We are to cut our hair above our shoulders.
> They are smoked with cedar and prayer
> So their Spirit can go freely to heaven.

We all pass the tradition down to the next generation, and they
    will learn the same way we did.
We all have heartbreaks and downfalls, but we look to God to
    help us through it, and make us stronger.
When we die, every person shall throw one handful of dirt into
    the casket, then we will bury.
Then no burdens shall be cast upon us and we will dance through
    the gates of heaven and be at peace with one another.
Amen.
In Loving Memory of our Grandfathers. Written with Pride.

Kateri, Kim, and Pam's prose gives us a glimpse of their spirituality that
is fashioned amid grief, tradition, and the shaping of their identity as
young women. It also raises questions about the sexism, racism, and
classism they may have experienced and how those experiences have
shaped their spirituality.

◆ ◆ ◆

This book is about the spirituality of adolescent girls such as Kateri,
Pam, and Kim, and the formative effects of race, class, and gender on
that spirituality. It began as an exploration of the rather barebones hy-
pothesis that the spirituality of adolescent girls of color, of lesbian and
working/poor white girls is affected by racism, classism, sexism, and
heterosexism. We see evidence of the effects of these forms of oppression in this volume's stories obtained by interviewers. By knowing of
this oppression, by listening to accounts of such experiences, leaders of
congregations and social agencies can more readily nurture a healthy
spirituality in girls with similar experiences.

Although Christian feminist, womanist, and mujerista theologians
have made great strides in articulating the effects of racism, sexism,
classism, and heterosexism on the spiritual lives of women, parallel
research and publications on adolescent girls has been minimal. This
book begins to fill that gap by giving adolescent girls a place in which

to articulate the effects of these forms of oppression on their spiritual selves.

This book explores adolescent female spirituality in light of systematized oppression in North American society. The experiences of girls from a variety of social locations are considered, including girls who come from rural, inner-city, suburban, economically deprived, and economically privileged situations. African American, Asian American, European American, Latina, and Native American girls' stories are here. Alongside them, interpreting and introducing the stories, feminist, mujerista, and womanist theologians and scholars engage in listening and dialogue with the adolescent girls with the goal of understanding how they make sense of their faith in light of the oppression they experience.

A Quick Literature Review

A host of feminist theologians have paved the way for critical reflection and discourse on the spirituality of women and the influence of sexism, racism, classism, and heterosexism. Mary Daly's *Beyond God the Father*, Rosemary Ruether's *Sexism and God-Talk*, Elisabeth Schüssler Fiorenza's *In Memory of Her*, Jacquelyn Grant's *White Women's Christ and Black Women's Jesus*, Ada María Isasi-Díaz and Yolanda Tarango's *Hispanic Women: Prophetic Voice in the Church*, Hyun Kyun Chung's *Struggle to Be the Sun Again*, and Audre Lorde's *Sister Outsider* are among the seminal books in the field of women's studies written from a theological, biblical, and religious perspective. Although these important contributions to feminist, womanist, and mujerista scholarship are used to discuss issues related to adolescent girls, because these works are primarily about women the process requires extensive extrapolation.

However, the disciplines of psychology, sociology, and education did contribute to scholarship about girls during the early days of feminism. Such works include Gisela Konopka's books, *The Adolescent Girl in Conflict*, published in 1966, and *Young Girls: A Portrait of Adolescence*, published in 1976. Konopka's first book sought to understand delinquent adolescent girls in juvenile justice institutions because they had experienced serious conflict with the existing society. She discovered that girls were bitter because of the changing cultural position of women; they resented the "double standard" for women but had little hope for transformation. The second book examined the attitudes, feelings, actions, hopes, and concerns of girls in the midst of change ten years after her initial research. With the 1992 publication of *Making Connections*, edited by Carol Gilligan, Nona Lyons, and Trudy Hanmer, and of *Meeting at the Crossroads*, the 1992 landmark publication about the turning points in girls' lives by Lyn Mikel Brown and Carol Gilligan, feminist, womanist, and mujerista theologians started to consider the particular needs of girls and the church's ministry with them. The 1994 bestseller *Reviving Ophelia* by Mary Pipher, which sought to understand the experiences of adolescent girls for whom she provided therapy, also influenced pastoral ministry with girls.

In 1996 Patricia Davis published *Counseling Adolescent Girls*, one of the first books that reflected theologically on girls and offered helpful information about the pastoral care and counseling with them. Davis offered some of the earliest research on girls' spirituality in chapter 3 of her book. Carol Lakey Hess, a practical theologian with expertise in educational ministry, gave us a feminist perspective on girls and women's development in congregations in her 1997 book titled *Caretakers of Our Common House: Women's Development in Communities of Faith*. The 2001 publication of *Beyond Nice: The Spiritual Wisdom of Adolescent Girls*, also by Patricia Davis, offers unparalleled scholarship in the area of girls' spirituality. Based on focused interviews with more than one hundred girls across the country, Davis offers a qualitative study of the meaning making of girls as they articulate their spiritual voices. Careful not to generalize her findings as universal for all adolescent girls, Davis constructs a healthy spirituality for a girl as one that "emanates from her relationship with God — the one she hopes will listen to her, value her, guide her, encourage her, and protect her." Also, a girl's spirituality is concerned with all the important relationships in her life that affirm the person she is becoming.[1]

In 1992 I began to investigate the political spirituality of African American adolescent girls in the civil rights movement. In this work I focused on Ruby Doris Smith and Joyce Ladner, two teenagers who made significant contributions to the black community in its struggle for freedom.[2]

In 1998 I examined the connection between sexuality and spirituality by analyzing the life story of Inga Marchand, a.k.a. "Foxy Brown," a teenage African American rap artist. In a scholarly paper I argued that Inga demonstrates a seamless self-understanding of her sexuality and her spirituality.

In "I Don't See Color," a chapter in my book *Trouble Don't Last Always: Emancipatory Hope among African American Adolescents* published in 2003, I used Davis's definition to examine the nature of loyalty in African American girls' spirituality, in particular the loyalty of members of two opposing female gangs. I explored black girls' loyalty in racially mixed groups, their individual racial prejudices and internalized racism, and their response to external forces of racism. Pat Davis's idea of a girl's spirituality as a relationship with God and those persons who affirm her becoming has broadened my understanding about loyalty as an aspect of black girls' spirituality.

Dori Baker's book *Doing Girlfriend Theology*, published in 2005, gives us a methodology for drawing out female adolescents' reflections on God and themselves, a methodology she names "story theology." Her method seeks to evoke "the text lying within girls' lives" as they come to voice in church and society. Auto/ethnography is her method of evoking girls' stories.

1. Patricia H. Davis, *Beyond Nice: The Spiritual Wisdom of Adolescent Girls* (Minneapolis: Fortress Press, 2001), 3.

2. I recently published a chapter entitled "Singing Hope and Practicing Justice: Emancipatory Hope Embodied in the Life of Ruby Doris Smith," in *Nurturing Child and Adolescent Spirituality: Perspectives from the World's Religious Traditions*, ed. Karen Marie Yust, Aostre N. Johnson, Sandy E. Sasso, and Eugene C. Roehlkepartain (New York: Roman and Littlefield, 2006).

A Word on Methodology

Following on this body of earlier work, this book is a qualitative study of the spirituality of a diverse group of female adolescents who are African American, European American, Korean American, Latina, and Native American, as well as a diverse group of lesbian college girls. These girls are pushed to the margins of North American society, where white middle-class and upper-class teenage girls are the model or ideal of what a teenage girl should be. These girls struggle to make sense of their experiences of injustice while clinging to and questioning God. This is not a definitive study of the effects of oppression on the spirituality of adolescent girls; its data cannot simply be generalized to larger populations of adolescent girls. Interviews with girls are treated as case studies as scholars theologically reflect on the intersection of girls' spirituality with oppression from racism, classism, sexism, and heterosexism.

All the girls interviewed for this book were between the ages of fifteen and eighteen, an age at which we assumed they have lived long enough to have a significant amount of experience upon which to reflect. This age cohort is also accustomed to abstract thinking and therefore able to think about their lives in relationship to their experiences of being female and of a minority. Their stories required interviews of an hour and a half to two hours conducted as focus groups or individual interviews. The interviews were same-sex, same-race matches between interviewer and interviewee except for interviews with girls who were intentionally selected for this project because of their sexual orientation as lesbian and their experiences of heterosexism. In this case Pat Davis, a heterosexual European American female, agreed to interview lesbian college girls because of her prior research experience with this population. The girls in this book represent the spectrum of socioeconomic groups, as do girls of color in general. However, the European American girls included are from working class/working poor communities only and it is only their experiences of classism and sexism that are explored.

Interview methods vary. I used a Life-Story in Metaphor method, which means that girls shared their stories using the metaphor of a song, and I listened for recurring themes. In similar fashion, Dori Baker used her method of girlfriend theology, where girls gather in groups along with female adults for three hours at a time over the course of several weeks to hear one another's stories. She listened for their understanding of God embedded in their stories. The other interviews for these chapters were conducted in focus groups or in individual clinical style using variations of the Life-Story in Metaphor protocol.

Definitions

The research that gave birth to this book sought to understand the effects of racism, classism, sexism, and heterosexism on the spirituality of adolescent females and the challenge of nurturing their healthy spirituality in light of these forms of oppression. The terms "spirituality," "racism," "classism," "sexism," and "heterosexism" are central to this project and merit clarity. By "spirituality" I mean girls' ways of knowing and being in the world that inform and shape their beliefs in God, the values they hold, and the practices they manifest. Beliefs include a girl's religious faith and her relationship to God or the Divine/Holy. Values include statements about what is right, wrong, good, and bad.[3] These beliefs, values, and practices intersect with their experiences of racism, sexism, classism, and heterosexism in ways that influence their unique ways of knowing and doing. We also understand an adolescent female's spirituality as her relationship with God or the Divine/Holy as she articulates that understanding. A girl's spirituality is formed in contexts that include home, school, and church, and her relationships in those contexts. Central to this understanding of a girl's spirituality are her relationships with God, family, friends, and all others who accompany and affirm her developing identity.[4]

---

3. Phil F. Carspecken, *Critical Ethnography in Educational Research: A Theoretical and Practical Guide* (New York: Routledge, 1996), 83.

4. Davis, *Beyond Nice*, 3.

Racism is a system of advantage that favors one group of persons economically, politically, psychologically, and socially at the expense of other groups.[5] "Racism is a *system* involving cultural messages and institutional policies and practices as well as beliefs and actions of individuals."[6] "White privilege" is the term that captures the concrete benefits derived from the unfair system of advantage that favors whites. Racial prejudice, the preconceived judgment or opinion about people of other races, perpetuates systems of white domination, but racial prejudice does not define racism.

Classism is an "economic system which creates excessive inequality" that favors a stratum of people with varying levels of economic power and puts at risk of not having their basic human needs met those with little or no economic power.[7] The stratum of an individual is based on a continuum that ranks people according to income, wealth, status, power, and a range of relative experiences that together define class identities. Ruling and owning classes are on the highest level of the stratum and working and poor classes are on the lowest level.[8] Practices compatible with class oppression also create systems of advantage based on class.

Sexism is the "societal/cultural, institutional, and individual beliefs and practices that privilege men, subordinate women, and denigrate women-identified values."[9]

Likewise, heterosexism is the "individual, institutional, and societal/cultural beliefs and practices based on the belief that heterosexuality

5. I was first introduced to the idea that racism is a system of advantage by Beverly Daniel Tatum, *Why Are All the Black Kids Sitting Together in the Cafeteria?* (New York: Basic Books, 1997), 7. Tatum refers to David Wellman, *Portraits of White Racism* (Cambridge: Cambridge University Press, 1977), chap. 1. After reading Wellman I adopted his more concrete definition of racism, which names the areas of advantage.

6. Tatum, *Why Are All the Black Kids Sitting Together in the Cafeteria?* 7.

7. Maurianne Adams, Lee Anne Bell, and Pat Griffin, *Teaching for Diversity and Social Justice* (New York: Routledge, 1997), 238.

8. Ibid.

9. Ibid., 162. Not only women's values but also their practices are denigrated by sexist individuals, 117.

is the only normal and acceptable sexual orientation.[10] Systems of advantage are created because of biases based on gender and sexual orientation.

◆ ◆ ◆

Such issues are the concern of a broad audience, including both academics in universities and seminaries and congregational leaders who care about the spirituality of girls and women. While research methods and analysis of data about girls' spirituality might be appealing to those in Christian education, pastoral care and psychology, sociology of religion, women's studies, and youth ministry, we hope that ordained pastors and laypersons in congregations who are concerned with good practices in ministry will find the stories of the girls in this book appealing and inspiring as well. I hope all readers will be drawn into the rich life-stories of these girls and the authors' meticulous theological reflection on the meaning these stories impart.

◆ ◆ ◆

So what can you expect in the pages that follow? The first chapter, entitled "I's Wide Shut: Eyelid Surgery as a Window into the Spirituality of Korean American Adolescent Girls," argues that Asian American girls literally embody in their faces, hair, and eyes the differences that are seen as inferior by the dominant culture. Their experiences are replete with issues around makeup, skin, and hair color and texture. Focusing on the stories of Korean American Girls, Su Yon meticulously examines the effects of eyelid surgery to reshape the eyes of girls and this phenomenon's severing of their connection to the sacred.

In chapter 2, "God and Grandmothers: Spiritual Values of Resistance to Racism among African American Adolescent Girls," I share stories of faith in God and relationships with significant women in the lives of middle-class African American girls. These stories show that among African American girls, God and grandmothers, mothers, and

10. Ibid., 146.

othermothers provide the spiritual presence and tenacity to negotiate white racism and demeaning stereotypes from other blacks. God cares and offers "amazing grace" in the midst of difficulties, making it possible for girls to persevere through difficulties caused by racism. Juxtaposed to these experiences and beliefs are those related to the uplift of other African American adolescents and the normalcy of selected material possessions.

In chapter 3, "From 'Wanton Girle' to the Woman Who Fell from the Sky: The Sacred Selves of Native American Girls," Laura E. Donaldson lifts up themes of coming of age among Native American girls in North America. These themes are shaped in relationship to the coming-of-age story of a young Powhatan girl, Pocahontas, who was revered in her community as an extraordinary girl from birth. Donaldson explores the place of ceremony, ritual, tradition, and history for Native girls whose life stories are shaped by the contradictions of identity and acceptance. The girls' stories do not conform to conventional definitions of adolescents. These stories, however, transcend essentialist constructs of development, identity, and spirituality.

In chapter 4, "Latina Adolescents: Sliding between Borders and the Yearning to Belong," Daisy Machado focuses on themes of identity and belonging in the stories of Latina adolescents who were born in the United Stated and of those who immigrated to the United States. Latinas struggle with belonging in North American culture, a struggle that entails and means different things for, say, Mexican American girls than it does for Colombian girls. Surrounding their struggles are issues of language, the political aspects of immigration and border crossing, as well as the struggles to "belong" in U.S. schools.

In chapter 5, "Love Letters in a Second-Hand Hope Chest: Working-Class White Girls Delaying Dreams and Expanding Souls," Dori Baker brings us the stories of white adolescent girls who are coming of age in the midst of economic downturn in Altavista, Virginia, where hourly wages continue to fall below the norm. Their struggles include dealing with absent fathers, betraying boyfriends, and backbiting girlfriends, as well as the chaos of poverty, teen pregnancy, and clergy sexual abuse.

An overriding theme of their stories is the disappointing search for intimacy, especially with fathers and boyfriends, in the midst of white privilege that creates a sort of cognitive dissonance for these girls. Given their background, it is perhaps not surprising — though none the less distressing — that the God they most readily articulate is a controlling monarch who threatens to punish bad choices with events causing tremendous loss. Yet the good news is that when images of God as nurturing, forgiving, loving, compassionate, and on the side of the downtrodden are offered, these girls readily entertain such images, despite contrary embedded theologies inherited from their families, churches, and culture.

In chapter 6, "Okay with Who I Am": Listening to Lesbian Young Women Talk about Their Spiritualities," Pat Davis shares the stories of lesbian college girls for whom the church often becomes a focus of pain, anger, and resentment because of the negative messages about homosexuality purveyed by preachers, youth ministers, and others purporting to speak for the faith about sexuality. The college-aged young women interviewed by Davis discuss the pain of being a member of a disfavored group in their churches. But they also talk constructively about ways they have attempted to change their faith communities, stay in relationship with those who are important, and find alternative ways of expressing their spiritualities — including embracing pagan religion, using religious themes in their art, and experiencing God in private devotion.

The concluding chapter, "Nurturing the Sacred Selves of Adolescent Girls," in revisiting the prominent themes from each chapter hopes to challenge those concerned about fostering a spirituality that is life-giving for girls who struggle with racism, classism, sexism, and heterosexism. The chapter also explores *realization, resistance, resilience,* and *ritual* as four essential components for nurturing a wholesome spirituality in adolescent girls. These components are couched in a metaphor of dancing that reflects a girl's healthy spirituality.

The nurture of girls' spirituality must be as specific as the stories in this book. That is to say, each girl needs to have her spirit nurtured in ways that address the realities she faces in North American society. The spiritual needs and realities of adults who will journey with them likewise demand specific attention and nurture. We hope that such a journey will offer opportunities for transforming girls' hard stories into emancipatory stories of God's love.

Chapter 1

I's Wide Shut

Eyelid Surgery as a
Window into the Spirituality of
Korean American Adolescent Girls

SU YON PAK

I was ten years old when I came to the United States. Our family landed in New York City, staking out a small apartment in a Greek enclave in Queens. Knowing no English, I took in this new world through my eyes. Quietly in the back of the classroom, or in front of the lunch line (I was the smallest in the class), I watched and studied how these new creatures lived and moved in this world. My eyes recorded the body movements, the goings on, and the life happenings. Like in the silent movies, I applied my own words and meaning to this world that I was both a part of and apart from at the same time. There were no sounds, no subtitles, no connection. In the quiet of my home, I would replay in my mind's eye all the events of the day. Pretty soon, I figured out who was flirting with whom, who struggled to keep his mouth shut, who did not do their homework. Then I realized that I was not the only one doing the watching. As the only Asian child in the class, and one of three in the school (one of whom was my sister), I was the object of the gaze of these students. They were watching me.

My first song in this new land was not "My Country, 'Tis of Thee" or "God Bless America" but a song of the playground. It was a song that I did not quite understand, except to know that it made me feel uncomfortable. With motions corresponding to the words, motions like pulling back the outer corners of their eyes with their finger, my playmates taught me this song: "Me Chinese, me Japanese, me dirty knees, me look at these." As they focused on my eyes, the window through which I understood this world, I began to realize that these eyes, the very instrument of my survival, had become an object of mockery and shame.

Reflecting upon my very first experience of racism as a ten-year-old, it became apparent to me that the way I was read by the gaze of the others affected my ability to be a self in the world. My eyes became the marker — the ethnic marker — that defined my being. My eyes became me. And to protect myself from this gaze that scrutinized, categorized, shamed, "normalized," and "disciplined" me, I began to create a mask.

Mask Dance:
"Reading" Asian American Adolescent Girls

Masks serve two functions: to hide oneself and to adopt another identity. In a Korean traditional mask dance named *tal-chum*, masks are used not only to personify a role or a character but also to identify that character's age, sex, and class. For example, black symbolizes an old man; red, a young man; white, a young woman. These colors are also used to identify directions and seasons: black for north and winter; red for south and summer. The masks of *yangban*, upper-class gentlemen, are identifiable by a deformity — harelips, a lopsided mouth, a distorted nose or squint eyes.[1] Developed by the common people during the Choson dynasty (1392–1910), *tal-chum* reflects the resistance they had toward their oppressors, the privileged class. The dance ridicules those in power through satire and parody. And by putting on the masks, the performers were able to speak truths about their situation

---

1. See Korean Overseas Culture and Information Service pamphlet, 1998.

through humor, music, and dance. Not only was the dance a form of entertainment; it was also a subversive activity.[2]

The power of this subversive act, however, is not only in the ability to ridicule those in power in the name of art, dance, and good communal fun. What makes it a particularly powerful act lies in the ability both to "put on" and "remove" the mask. Putting on the mask allows actors' to resist to oppressive forces, but taking it off reestablishes them in the reality of their identity. Yet the permanent mask loses its subversive power when it cannot be removed. The identity of the mask eventually becomes the identity of the person as he or she is continually "read" as the mask.

In a culture that readily categorizes and defines a person's identity by the way they are "read," racial features or ethnic markers that visually identify Koreans and Korean Americans (eyes, hair, nose, and skin) are "read" to stereotype and marginalize — to make them the "other." When compared to the prevailing standard of beauty as defined by the dominant culture in this consumerist society, these ethnic markers become "disfigurement" that needs "correction" or, in Foucault's language, "discipline." Here, I draw on Foucault's analysis of power to assist in understanding the complexity of this dynamic. Foucault moves away from a simplistic understanding of the oppressor/oppressed dichotomy where the oppressor possesses power and the oppressed are denied power. He suggests the dynamic is more subtle than that: "There is no need for arms, physical violence, material constraints. Just a gaze. An inspecting gaze, a gaze which each individual under its weight will end by interiorizing to the point that he is his own overseer, each individual thus exercising this surveillance over, and against himself."[3] In other words, the power of the gaze lies in its ability to make individuals internalize, self-inspect, and self-discipline. In order to protect herself from the gaze, a girl therefore puts on a mask.

2. For further discussion of the Korean Mask Dance, see *Essays on Minjung*, ed. Korea Theological Study Institute (Seoul: Korea Theological Study Institute, 1984).
3. Michel Foucault, "The Eye of Power" in *Power/Knowledge: Selected Interviews and Other Writings*, ed. Colin Gordon (New York: Pantheon, 1980), 155.

Because of this dynamic of inspection–protection–masking, identity formation as well as spiritual formation for Korean American adolescent girls is a profoundly embodied process.[4] The body "feels" the "disfigurement," and it consciously or unconsciously presents itself to the world physically, so as to mask the "disfigurement." The mask becomes an identity projected outward, and then projected back onto it as people "read" the body as Asian American. The most significant symbolic "disfigurement" for Korean American adolescent girls (and women as well) is the eyes. The mask here is the "disciplining" of the eyes so as to "normalize" them to a Western standard of beauty.

For me, the practice of disciplining took the form of applying makeup. My teenage years were marked by hours in front of the mirror with my sister trying to make our eyes more "Western." This included taping thin strips of Scotch tape along the eyelids to accentuate the crease and trying various types of eyeliners and eye shadows so that my eyes would look larger and rounder. Our bodies are the locus, the canvas, and sometimes the battleground of identity. But our bodies are also where we experience God. We learn, at an early age, that spiritual practices — such as praying, singing, and healing — are highly embodied. The body is where spirituality is made manifest. So in order to study the effects of racism, sexism, classism, and heterosexism on the spirituality of Korean American adolescent girls, we need to understand how their bodies are "read" and "disciplined" in ways that are particular to them.

Spirituality, "a soul force energy that connects and relates human beings to the Divine, self, and community,"[5] is an "act" that demands

4. Patricia Davis reminds us that spirituality is embodied for everyone. In her discussion about sexuality and spirituality, she writes, "Sexuality is naturally connected to spirituality. People are embodied spirits — without our bodies we cease to exist as human beings." *Beyond Nice: The Spiritual Wisdom of Adolescent Girls* (Minneapolis: Fortress Press, 2001), 82–83. But for Asian American adolescents, this plays itself out in a more negative context. It is being seen as "other" that forces them to deal with their bodies.

5. Kathleen Talvacchia, *Critical Minds and Discerning Hearts: A Spirituality of Multicultural Teaching* (St. Louis: Chalice Press, 2003), 11.

intimacy with God and others.[6] But this intimacy cannot be achieved while wearing a mask. Any intimacy requires the removal of the mask. At the same time, a mask is a protection against the harsh elements of life. It is a necessity for survival. Given this paradoxical reality, these questions surface: How do Korean American adolescent girls negotiate this paradox of masking and unmasking? What helps do they have from the church, community, family, and society? What implication does this paradox have for their spirituality?

This chapter is an attempt to answer these questions. First, using the metaphor of the mask and other theoretical perspectives, I analyze the practice of eyelid surgery and its relationship to identity formation. Then, in the "Womenspeak" section, I explore experiences of three Asian American women, the pressures on them, and their decisions about eyelid surgery. Finally, in the "Girlspeak" section, Korean American adolescent girls voice their struggle to come to terms with their embodied spirituality and identity. I conclude this chapter with questions for further investigation.

The Mask of *Ssal-ga-pul* (Double Eyelid)

Many Asian people have eyelids with no visible lid folds. It is referred to as "single eyes." The essence of double eyelid surgery is to create beautiful double eyes without altering the ethnic charm of the Oriental. — Dr. Chettawut Tulayaphanich, M.D., plastic surgeon[7]

Currently, I am looking into getting cosmetic surgery done on my eyes. Life is about self-improvement... It is [about] feeling good about myself. — Maria "Rebba" Estante from *Western Eyes*[8]

When I was six years old, they saw me as a young Asian, they said, "chink, poor, dirty girl." And of course if that's the way they

---

6. Davis, *Beyond Nice*, x.

7. *www.chet-plasticsurgery.com/double_eyelid.html.*

8. *Western Eyes*, directed by Ann Shin (Montreal: National Film Board of Canada, 1999).

perceive you, you begin believing it. I am re-creating myself. I am balancing East and West together. I want to get it [the eyelid surgery] done because I want to feel better. I want to feel better.

— Sharon from *Western Eyes*

According to statistics made available by the American Society of Plastic Surgeons (ASPS), there were 233,334 blepharoplasties (eyelid surgeries) performed in 2004 in the United States alone. The frequency of this procedure has increased by 125 percent since 1992.[9] Of this figure, the highest demand was among women of Korean, Chinese, and Japanese descent.[10] In South Korea, some 40 percent of girls and women undergo blepharoplasty,[11] most commonly among older girls in high school before attending college. Blepharoplasty, traditionally performed for medical reasons for patients with excess eyelid skin that interferes with the proper functioning of their eyes, has in recent years been requested by Asian American women to cosmetically create double eyelids.

Around 50 percent of women of Asian descent are known to have "singled-lidded" eyes, meaning eyes that have no crease. Due to the position and amount of fat under the eyelid, Asian eyes tend to have a fuller look (some call it "puffy"), without a crease. By removing "excess" fat and thus creating a fold, "double eyelids" give a sense of having larger eyes. Usually performed on an outpatient basis, this procedure takes between one and three hours. Under local anesthesia, the surgeon makes a cut along the upper eyelid and removes a sliver of skin, obicularius muscle, as well as some of the fat underneath. Then the eyelid is reattached in a slightly different position so as to form a crease. Generally, it takes about two weeks for the swelling to go down and heal.

---

9. For a fuller statistical picture, go to the American Society of Plastic Surgeon's website: *www.plasticsurgery.org/public_education/2004Statistics.cfm*. Blepharoplasty is the third most requested cosmetic surgery for women and one of three most requested for Asian American women, the other two being nose construction and breast augmentation.

10. Shirley Lin, "In the Eye of the Beholder?: Eyelid Surgery and Young Asian-American Women," *www.alternet.org/wiretap/10557*, March 6, 2001.

11. Junhee Kim, *www.seoulselection.com/streetwise_read.html?cid=1482*.

But it can take up to six months before the final position of the crease settles. Medical complications of this surgery include double vision, loss of vision, and the inability to shut the eyes completely.[12] The cost for this surgery is anywhere between $1,500 and $3,000, the 2004 U.S. national average being $2,523. Many Korean American girls and women go back to Korea to get the surgery done because it costs less and surgeons there are more skilled in performing the surgery on Korean faces.[13]

Why has there been an epidemic of eyelid surgery in recent years? In North American culture as well as other cultures, the body is a text to be read and interpreted. For each body part, there is a commonly understood "script" or "subtext" that interprets that body part. For example, a long neck equals elegance, full lips equal sexy, fat equals lazy, etc.[14] In this culture then, the question becomes understanding in what ways race-specific features get scripted and how that scripting affects the self-image and identity of the woman with those features.

Lisa Jervis, in her article "My Jewish Nose," articulates the pressure she feels from her mother to get her "honker" fixed so as to make her "more gentile" (read, "genteel") and "whiter." The cultural "script" written about a big Jewish nose is the stereotypical Jewish woman — loud and pushy, which are qualities that girls should not have. She writes, "Ditch the physical and emotional ties with your ethnicity in one simple procedure: Bob your nose, and become feminine in both mind and body."[15] By advocating and sometimes forcing rhinoplasty

---

12. For further information on the anatomy of Asian eyes and surgical procedures, complete with before-and-after photographs visit: *www.drmeronk.com/asian-eyelid.html.*

13. Anecdotally, it is so popular in South Korea that almost every other house in the affluent Kang Nam area in Seoul is a plastic surgeon's office. A *New York Times* article on June 17, 2004, entitled "Beijing Journal: Beauty Contestant Fights for Right of Self-Improvement," reports on the epidemic of plastic surgery clinics to produce "artificial beauties" in China. This article focuses on a young woman named Yang Yuan who was disqualified from the Miss Intercontinental Beijing beauty contest because she underwent cosmetic surgery that altered her eyes, nose, mouth and chin. Yang has filed a lawsuit against the contest claiming that her rights were violated.

14. Rebecca Walker, foreword, to *Body Outlaws: Young Women Write about Body Image and Identity,* ed. Ophira Edut (Seattle: Seal Press, 2000), xiii.

15. Lisa Jervis, "My Jewish Nose," in Walker, *Body Outlaws,* 64.

on their offspring, Jewish mothers and grandmothers attempt to expunge ethnic markers from their daughter's bodies in order for them to conform to the "white" "Caucasian" standard of beauty celebrated by this culture.[16]

Just as a Jewish nose implied a certain stereotype, so too do many other cultures experience cultural scripting of their features. For Asians, single-lidded eyes have a cultural "script." "Small, slanty" eyes, "sleepy" eyes have negative behavioral characteristics attached to them. Negative racial stereotypes of women of Asian descent as "docile, passive, slow witted, and unemotional" are associated with ethnic-specific facial features such as their eyes. This stereotype is internalized by many Asian American women, causing them to consider removing the ethnic marker that implies, not just their ethnicity, but the negative traits associated with their ethnicity.[17]

Furthermore, for racial ethnic minority women, this cultural script is complicated by white feminists' downplaying of physical appearance and beauty. For one Korean American woman, Elisa, rewriting this cultural script is a neocolonial practice. She goes ahead with the surgery and then reflects on that practice. She grew up a tomboy who wanted to get into the "whiteboy club," so when her parents gave her the "feminizing/colonizing tool called an eyelid glue pen,"[18] she used it. After high school graduation, when her parents offered to pay for eyelid surgery for her, she got it done. Reflecting on this passage from being a tomboy who did not even believe in using makeup, to using the eyelid glue pen, and ultimately having eyelid surgery, she asked herself why she did it. She writes:

> Because I had been programmed to value beauty but to also shun it as trivial. . . . I was informed by western standards of beauty which bound me, and by white feminism which was supposed

---

16. Ibid., 64.
17. Eugenia Kaw, "Medicalization of Racial Features: Asian American Women and Cosmetic Surgery," *Medical Anthropology Quarterly* 7, no. 1 (1993): 74–89.
18. Elisa Paik, "Eye-dentity Crisis," in *yello* 1 (1998): 31.

to liberate me but made me more confused. . . . I felt that I, an Asian woman with hooded eyes, could *not* be beautiful by western standards but that I should try — and should then feel guilty about being so frivolous. . . . So I spiraled deeper into the sewage of self-hate, ashamed of myself for not being a white boy, for not being beautiful, and for even trying.[19]

Critiquing both the "norm" of white culture and the white feminist critique of that norm, Elisa comes to see the eyelid surgery as a tool of cultural colonialism — not dissimilar to military colonization. Although she does not regret the surgery since her eyes have "literally shaped [her] identity, and the ways which [she sees,]" she does realize that she has been "pierced by something painful."[20]

Eugenia Kaw, in her article "Medicalization of Racial Features: Asian American Women and Cosmetic Surgery," discovers that the types of plastic surgery American women undergo are race-specific. White women tend to choose surgery that is motivated by a need to look more beautiful as a *woman*. They opt for liposuction, breast augmentation, or wrinkle removal. In a culture that worships youth and slimness, white women try to fit that mold of a beautiful young woman. But Asian American women opt for surgery that removes "conventional markers of racial identity."[21] They most often request double-eyelid surgery. This suggests that while white women's bodies are primarily read according to how womanly they are perceived to be, Asian American women's bodies are read primarily as to how stereotypically Asian they appear. The one is filtered by gender, the other by race. Furthermore, Kaw insists that the medical system, capitalizing on consumerist values, promotes and perpetuates this racist notion of beauty. "By maintaining the idea that beauty should be every woman's goal [and] . . . by promoting a beauty standard that requires that certain

---

19. Ibid., 32.
20. Ibid., 33.
21. Kaw, "Medicalization of Racial Features," 75.

racial features of Asian American women be modified,"[22] the medical system, a producer of norms, "encourage[s] Asian American women to mutilate their bodies to conform to an ethnocentric norm."[23]

Drawing on anthropological studies on decoration, ornamentation, and scarification of the body, Kaw highlights two perspectives: a practice of celebration or of mutilation. Seen as a practice of celebration, scarification of the body can be an expression of belonging to a community or society and an affirmation of *being in* the body. On the other hand, seen as a practice of mutilation, it can be an expression of alienation in a community or society and a negation of the body produced by unequal power relationships. While she can imagine how some might believe that undergoing double-eyelid surgery for Asian American women can be a celebration of belonging to this society, like a rite of passage, she argues that this surgical transformation is an act of self, body, and societal alienation. Although the subjects she studied did not consider their surgery as acts of mutilation, it is clear that they all viewed their "given" bodies as undesirable, producing a sense of marginality. While some women deny that the surgery is to conform to any standard of beauty — feminine or Western — most women agreed that they wanted to look their best, meaning less Asian.

Moreover, Kaw cites that the reason for the surgery in her subject was never purely aesthetic. This is tied up with their sense of marginal status. They view having less-Asian eyes as higher, prestigious status, as having "symbolic capital." However, this desire for improvement does not challenge the cultural and institutional structures that marginalize Asian American women and render them powerless. This "normalization" further confirms and perpetuates the undesirability of Asian features, and thus Asians themselves, which in turn strengthens the unjust structures that marginalize Asian American women to begin with. Moreover, this "normalization" for Asian American women is a double process: "conforming to patriarchal definitions of feminine

22. Ibid. 75.
23. Ibid., 75.

and to Caucasian standards of beauty."[24] Asian American women who undergo surgery are opting for an individual response to a structural oppression. And of course, the individualistic and freedom-orientated consumer nature of American society assists in opting for this response. For Kaw, the medical institution, using its authority of scientific rationality and technological efficiency, manipulates the racist, sexist, and capitalist culture to promote and benefit from the mutilation of Asian American women's bodies.

What Kaw does not engage in her article is class analysis of this beauty project. A cultural script, and its negative impact on one's status that is imposed on Asian American women's bodies, applies to all Asian American women living in this society. But the *ability* to rewrite the script and do something about it is tied to economic privilege, i.e., class. For poor women, the "symbolic capital" of "Western eyes" is not just symbolic; it is material reality. In the absence of material ability to rewrite the cultural script, how do poor Asian American women respond to this negative cultural script? What are their rewriting strategies? Although this chapter does not explicitly address these questions from the perspective of poor Korean American women, economic analysis must be highlighted even in the absence of those who can speak from this perspective.

Whether or not one agrees with Kaw's cultural and poststructuralist analysis of the "eye project," what is evident is the feeling of ambivalence in Asian American women and girls about having their eyes done. Pressure from mothers, cultural representations of beauty, and white feminists' dismissal of giving attention to physical appearance are some of the realities that Asian American women and girls live with on a daily basis. These realities inform their self-image and self acceptance. They are complex and complicated. As Susan Bordo, drawing on Marxist and later Foucauldian perspectives, suggests, it is through the bodily practices and habits of everyday life,

---

24. Ibid. 78.

more than conscious explicit instruction, that we learn how to be-
have "appropriately" for our gender, race, and social class (and sexual
orientation, I would add). Furthermore, it is through these practices
and bodily habits that the culture claims the "direct grip."[25] This perspective helps us to see the relationship between the "direct grip"/gaze
and the eyelid surgery. Through the daily habit of gluing the eyelids
and gazing in the mirror, with the new double-lidded eyes (either by
surgery or daily gluing), we learn our place in society. This mask, and
the habit of putting on this mask, becomes an act of containment and
control carried out by oneself; it becomes a tool of self-containment
and self-control. With time, this mask becomes a permanent one that
cannot be removed. Being in the body in this way has a profound
affect on one's spirituality and self identity. This is especially poignant
and problematic in adolescence since it is a time of "putting on" and
"taking off" of identities/masks in search of an authentic self. How do
Korean American adolescent girls negotiate this?

Girlspeak on
Embodied Spirituality and Identity

This section gives voice to what some Korean American adolescents
are thinking about racism, sexism, classism, and spirituality, albeit in
an indirect way. I have interviewed four Korean American adoles-
cent/young adult girls aged sixteen to twenty-one, who (I found out
during the interview), have not undergone eyelid surgery. I have also
incorporated in this section interviews from *Western Eyes*, a documentary about Korean American adolescents/young adults and their
experiences of having the eyelid surgery done. This documentary was
used at the beginning of the interview as a conversation starter.

The four girls were interviewed together. They are from a Korean
American United Methodist Church in Atlanta, and all live in middle-
class suburban neighborhoods. Three girls have both parents living

---

25. Susan Bordo, *Unbearable Weight: Feminism, Western Culture, and the Body*
(Berkeley: University of California Press, 1993), 16.

with them; one lives with her mother, her parents being divorced. They all speak a mixture of English and Korean, "Konglish," at home. One was born in South Korea and three were born in the United States. As a group, we watched *Western Eyes* as a way of getting into the topic of eyelid surgery.

Western Eyes

"In a culture where the standard of beauty is unyielding, what happens to women who feel they don't fit in? What goes on inside a woman who is desperately unhappy with how she looks on the outside?"[26] questions Ann Shin, the filmmaker of *Western Eyes*.

Western Eyes is a documentary about two Asian Canadian young adult females in search of beauty and racial identity. Sharon is a Korean Canadian woman in her early twenties, whose parents immigrated to Alberta, Canada, where she was born. She is contemplating blepharoplasty. Maria Estante, "Rebba," was born in the Philippines. She is contemplating both rhinoplasty and blepharoplasty. They believe that their Asian looks, specifically their eyes, get in the way of who they really are and how people see them.

The filmmaker, Ann Shin, attempts to look beneath the skin to painful experiences that shaped and formed their images of themselves to see underlying reasons why they want to have their faces altered. Recalling the hatred she experienced as a child, Sharon feels that her outward appearance and specifically her Asian appearance was the cause of her trauma. She says, "When I was six years old, they saw me as a young Asian. They said, 'Chink, poor dirty girls.' And of course, if that's the way they perceive you, you begin believing it." Rebba talks about being Filipina in the colonial context. "In a culture that has been dominated for three hundred years, there is a lot of race trauma. The more American or Australian you look, the more beautiful you are, the more Spanish you look, the more beautiful you are." For Rebba, her plastic surgery will help her connect to her Spanish blood: she has

---

26. Promotional material on the back of the video cover.

a Spanish great grandmother. "I want to look in the mirror and see who I really am."

Both Sharon and Rebba struggle with why they want to alter their face. Introduced to blepharoplasty by her mother, Sharon talks about growing up grasping for an identity by "trying on" various images of herself at the clothing stores. "You know, before, in my younger years, I tried to model myself as the new up-and-coming model. I would go through each and every hanger and look at different possibilities. And it would give me potential to imagine, to imagine another place." This "trying on" of outfits and identities — like putting on masks — was a way not only to imagine but also to escape from her painful reality. For Rebba, it is about self-improvement and about feeling good about herself. She says, "I could spend $5,000 [on surgery] and feel better and feel more confident in social situations and not so insecure and self-conscious, or I can go to therapy."

The need to "feel better" is shared by Sharon as well: "I am re-creating myself. I am balancing East and West together. I want to get it done because I want to feel better. I want to feel better." However, the night before surgery, Sharon reflects: "There was a note of sadness that hit me today. You know, a snake shed its skin. That's how I am feeling a little bit. It's a new beginning, a new cycle. I am torn between having the surgery and not having the surgery. I need to think about this . . . about what my intentions are."

Sharon never explicitly shares what her true intentions are for having the surgery done. The pain of the trauma prevents her from opening up fully to be vulnerable to the gaze of the camera lens. But after the surgery, even though she feels that it was a success, when Ann Shin asks her the true reasons for getting her "eyes done," she replies:

There's some forces that drive me to do this. It's very, almost Frankenstein-like having to cut into yourself and cut and pull. Somewhat, I wouldn't say that it's masochistic? But being black and blue isn't a healthy thing. However, that's a process you need to go through. I am still peeling away all those layers. All those different disguises. I remember this so vividly. When I was six years old, my brother, my grandfather, and I were waiting at the bus stop. Hey, there's some chinks over there. They started throwing things at us. I was like, "Why are you throwing rocks at us?" I was, like, so helpless. . . . I really don't want to film this . . . I never tell anyone . . . because hate, being subjected to that form of hate, like, what can you do? . . . I am coming to realize that I was very much affected by that form of hate. . . . I took somewhat the easy way out. But that's something that I'll need to deal with. To be so self-absorbed, narcistic [sic], it's destructive.

Somewhere in a secret chamber of her heart, Sharon knows the relationship between being subjected to this form of hatred and body mutilation. She calls it "some forces" that drive her to do this. She is coming to terms with the superficiality of removing a mask that is only skin deep. In removing one mask, she is replacing it with another — a permanent one. *Western Eyes* is a probing examination of beauty and perception: "how we see; how we are seen; how we see how we are seen."[27]

Group Interview

The four interviewees were asked to reflect on and converse about the following questions after viewing *Western Eyes*:

1. Does the film evoke a story for you? What is that story?
2. How do you make your decision about clothing, makeup, and your body image? What/who helps you to make that decision (magazines, e.g., *Cosmo Girl, Seventeen;* peers; church; mother, siblings, family; movies, etc.)? Do you experience any conflicts between different influences (e.g., peers and family)?

Prior to our interview, I did not know whether any of the girls had had the eyelid surgery. Since the surgery is rather a common phenomenon

27. Ibid.

in the Korean American community, there was a high probability either that one of the girls had surgery or that one of them knew someone in their family or circle of friends who had had it done. I needed to be careful about the questions so I would not immediately put them on the spot. The purpose of viewing a documentary as an entry point for further discussion was to ensure some safe way to talk about an otherwise very contentious issue. Furthermore, the questions needed to be focused *less* on the eyelid surgery specifically and *more* on the relationship between the body image and spirituality as a whole. For instance, I did not want to ask, "What do you think about *ssang-ga-pul* (double eyelid) surgery?" This question would put the girls on the spot in ways that might evoke shame or a need to save face. During the interview, I challenged them to think about the role of the church or Christian faith in the way they see and carry themselves, their bodies, and their image.

I was struck by how quickly the girls claimed that they could not relate to Sharon's experience. They wondered if the Canadian scene is very different from the United States. These girls did not have the experience of racism that the film depicted. Susan,[28] a sixteen-year-old, said:

> I guess it's different for me 'cause of where I grew up. I never got called racial slurs or anything.

Three girls quickly jumped in to say that they do not approve of plastic surgery. They thought Sharon looked fine the way she was. Joyce, a twenty-one-year-old, said:

> I can't really relate to the film. I don't approve of plastic surgery or anything like that. 'Cause once you find something that you don't like in your body, like on your face or whatever, you're going to find another thing like that's bothering you and you're going to try to fix that.

---

28. All names are pseudonyms to protect confidentiality.

Christina, another sixteen-year-old, stated matter-of-factly:

> She should be grateful. God made her that way. Just be grateful for what you have. I think this generation is different. I think the Asian look is actually popular. There's lots of Asians . . . like Lucy Liu. . . .

Joyce dismisses racial slurs as being ignorant:

> I remember my sister actually saying that she was called a "chink" once. It's funny that people would think, just because we have black hair and a flat face we get called "chink." People who say the word don't even know what it means. Chink is that little tiny crack. You know, it's like, come on, dude, do you know about what you are saying?

I pushed Joyce a bit. I asked whether her sister talked about this incident with her. In my experience, it is much easier to brush it off as ignorance, but when we talk about it, we realize that it has actually affected us much more than we would like to admit. Joyce said:

> Yeah, [we talked about it]. I mean but I feel like it wasn't such a big deal because we were able to get over that, you know, and it wasn't like it scarred us for life. Or you know, I mean of course it impacts us like, oh gosh, people are so ignorant, you know.

It seemed from the interview thus far that the girls were all in agreement about problematizing plastic surgery and not having the same experience of racism as Sharon in the film. Joyce said:

> I think it's weird how something that was done to her as a child stuck with her so much that she would have to change her appearance to make that inner turmoil go away, I guess. And, I don't know, it doesn't seem like she's happier because of it. It seems like she's worse off now because she changed herself because of all that pressure.

Because the girls did not really seem to be able to relate to this film, I asked if they knew of anyone else in their family or among their friends who has gone through eyelid surgery. Then sixteen-year-old Andrea spoke out hesitantly:

> I actually did glue on my eyes to make the *ssang-ga-pul* [double eyelid]. But I'm kind of a hypocrite. I don't really agree with doing surgery. But then I would think enhancing your appearance is bad. I know there is, God made you this way, this way and this way. So you should be grateful and there's nothing wrong with looking the way you do. But even with losing weight or if you're working out, you're still enhancing your appearance without doing surgery, you know. So where is the line where surgery is wrong but working out is okay?

Challenging the simplistic right-wrong answers to the ways in which we "adorn" and take care of our bodies, Andrea recounts the reason why she decided to glue her eyelids to create double-lidded eyes. For her, it was not pressure from others telling her that she was ugly. It began more with the internal pressure to look cool, her own desire to become a model, "just trying to fit into the whole set appearance." Although it began during a certain stage of wanting to look cool, it then became a habit for her even though now she doesn't really agree with it.

To get more explicitly at their spirituality regarding their self-image and identity, I asked them to identify who, what, and where they find help in making decisions about clothes, makeup, and hair. Do they look to magazines, family, church, or the media to help them with how they will present themselves? Their responses were all varied and individual. Susan said:

> I actually don't give in to the media. I mean, I don't want to look like anybody else. I just want to look like me. I don't put on makeup. I wear something that's like, comfortable. I don't wear heels to school, and it's kinda stupid. I don't give in to the models

and the media 'cause, like, I don't think models are pretty. I think they look ridiculously skinny, and then, like, I just, I don't give into it and I don't have guidelines for the way I look either. I just wear what's in the closet.

When I pressed her about what helps her to make decisions about what clothes to buy, she replied:

If it fits, it fits. I mean, if it's a good price. I don't like shopping at the mall anymore because everything is expensive and plus it's . . . everybody wears it! When I was in middle school, I used to wear plain old Gap clothes. But then I see someone wearing the same thing. I really don't like people wearing the same clothes as I do and so now I just shop at thrift stores and stuff and like, it's just so . . . if it fits, it fits. I don't really care the way I look.

Andrea likes to mix and match her own style. She likes "funky stuff" like Elle Girls and Betsy Johnson. She likes to design her own clothes. Christina always tries to dress "trendy." When asked what she meant by "trendy," she replied:

I guess I follow my sister. She's stylish. I always try to be sort of different, sort of, like, I don't know, it's not really different, but I try to wear something that stands out.

Joyce, on the other hand, prefers "mainstream" designs. When asked what she meant by "mainstream," she said:

Last year, or like in my summers, I usually worked at clothing stores, and that's where I've gotten my clothes and that's the style. Last summer, I worked at Abercrombie & Fitch so a lot of my clothes are from Abercrombie. . . . I go to Emory and so it's very upper class too, um, just looking at other people and what they wear too. Just like what my friends wear.

Their favorite clothing store included thrift stores, Urban Outfitters, Fossil, and The Gap. There was an interesting interaction among the three sixteen-year-old girls where one girl declared that she liked to wear boys' tees. This remark brought on teasing from another girl:

"You're a gangster."

"No, I'm not!"

"I listen to rap." [The group laughs.]

For the first time in our interview, this gentle teasing brought out the relationship between what you wear and who you are. The image "gangster" or *kkang pae* is a very common image in the Korean/Korean American community where one's refusal to conform to a certain way of dressing is very often labeled "gangster." For example, when I was a teenager, at my church, there was a group of girls who wore blue jeans and T-shirts to church. They were called *chung bah ji*, which meant "blue jeans." They were associated with a certain kind of gangster-like behavior and social life. We were taught not to associate with them because we were "nice girls." For me, the acculturation I got at church had a profound impact on who I was and wasn't to be. Connecting a certain way of dressing to a behavior that is then attributed to an identity is society's mechanism for both socialization and social control.

In order to see how church life affected their understanding of their self-image, I asked: What are some of the messages you get from your church about body image and self-image? The three sixteen-year-olds were articulate about what their church taught about who they are. Susan said:

I guess the thing about God making us different and all that. . . . In one sermon, the pastor was talking about when God created man, He said, "It was good." So I mean, like, yeah, we're good. The reason why I don't really give in to media and all is because God did make us all different and so we don't need to try to be somebody else. Church at times helps with that, with the way I look at myself and the way I should carry myself, 'cause, I mean, it is very important to live your life, you know, as Christian and all that.

Christina jumped in:

Remember like you said, like our body is a temple of worship for God. So like, keeps you or like me from doing stuff to my body, something like tattoos or like piercing, yeah. I remember I used to want three piercings in my ear and then my parents are telling me you shouldn't put holes in your body and like that's true 'cause it is like a temple for God and it is reinforced in the church.

Andrea agreed, saying: "Our life isn't about us. We live for God. He thinks we're beautiful, so. . . . "

Trying to get at the conflicting messages we get from church, media, family, and friends, I asked them, "How do you deal with conflict when God thinks you're beautiful but others don't? We all think that God thinks that we're beautiful and God has made us this way, but sometimes maybe we haven't experienced feeling beautiful. How does one deal with that conflict?" Quite unexpectedly, this question brought us back to the topic of plastic surgery. Joyce said:

In high school, I was pretty image conscious. I would make sure I was dressed so someone would be, "Oh you're dressed really cute today." I would always want that one compliment, at least one compliment a day, and then on the inside I'd be like, "Oh I'm so ugly. I'm so ugly." I'd say that and my sister would quote the Bible saying, "You know God made you. You're wonderfully and fearfully made," or something. I never listened to her. And okay, that's what the Bible says and not what I think and a lot of times I've struggled with that whole appearance thing. Like the girls said, the Bible is a big support but it's kinda funny because you know we've grown up in the Korean society. Koreans are also very image conscious. I was reading a magazine and it said that the Korean in South Korea was one of the most [plastic] surgery people. Yeah, plastic surgery, like they've done it and it's like, you know all eyes and nose ... go figure.

The conversation moved from the conflict between the Bible/church teachings and society to the conflict within the church. The girls were all in agreement about the conflicting messages they get when they go to church. While the Bible says looks should not matter, the church members, particularly women of the church, are very critical of the way girls look. Joyce continued:

Korean people are very blunt and okay, they're either going to tell you you're ugly or you're pretty. And when they say that you're pretty, you say, "Yes! I made it to the A-list!" You know, it's funny. The pastor says, "You know God says this and this and this." But then you have your surrounding community saying "No. You're not this." You know we wear our Sunday best and make sure it's the best out of everyone else. You know, it's funny to come to church where you're supposed to not care about these things but it's very prominent.

In an attempt to understand the pressure this generation gets from the older generation about image, I asked them if they feel pressure from their parents' generation to dress or be a certain way. Andrea and Christina implied that they used to be more conscious, but now they have "grown up." They do not have the same need to "be cool." On the other hand, Susan was very vocal about never caring what other people thought about her. Her mother does not tell her what to wear and has always told her to be herself.

You should be comfortable with who you are and I mean, like, I'm comfortable with who I am. I don't give in to what other people think about me and all that. So you know, that's about it!

The final conversation moved in the direction of how Asian Americans are portrayed in the media and in society. They spoke about commodification of Asian-ness — looks, food, clothes — which takes away their identity and agency to be who they are. They feel like they are being told what Asian-ness is by the dominant culture. The following conversation highlights this complex dilemma:

Joyce: Actually, in South America, Asian men are the hot commodity.

Andrea: Well, Asian women are kinda "in" right now. Like Asian clothing and Asian food. When you look in ads there's a lot more Asian girls.

Joyce: But it's funny because they only use one type of Asian face. I feel like they use a lot of times that one typical Asian look, like, the slant eyes and like, they call that oriental. I was reading this magazine. I still have my *Seventeen* magazines from high school. I was looking through it and there was "how you do Asian eyes." And there are these girls and they have very slanted eyes, really, slanted eyes and I'm like, "That's not my eyes...."

Interviewer: It seems like they are telling you that now you can look Asian but you can only look this type of Asian 'cause that's kind of the model Asian look, but you say you disagree.

Christina: [To say that] most Asians have slanted eyes...just like us saying, are you like Indian, or Mexican or being ignorant about other cultures. Am I going totally off the subject?

Joyce: I'm not getting you.

Christina: I don't know what I'm trying to say, but like, whenever people call us Chinese or Japanese instead of Korean, that's just like us saying like are you Mexican when they're really Spanish or something or saying are you Indian when they're Pakistan [*sic*]. It's just us being ignorant too. I don't know, yeah....

As these conversations reveal, there are connections to be made about self-image, what the church teaches and preaches, and what the Korean American community and the larger society value. They point out yet another commodification of Asian-ness parading itself as "positive" or valued that becomes another straitjacket into which these girls are supposed to fit. The representation of Korean American females in the media and in the larger culture has a profound effect on the self-image and ultimately the spirituality of these adolescent girls. The desire to look "cool," to be like the models and yet different from anyone else, is paradoxical. The desire to homogenize (i.e., to look white, look thin, conform to the "norm") and the desire to be different (i.e., clothes that stand out) co-exist. The struggle to belong in a community and individuate at the same time, tasks certainly appropriate for adolescence, become more complicated for these girls due to their race.

Furthermore, there is a suspicious absence of class in their conversations. Class seemed "assumed." In an immigrant community, class is a sticky issue. A person's class status can change overnight due to immigration. A well-respected medical doctor in Korea can be a manual worker in a green grocer's with no health benefits in the United States. In the Korean American immigrant community, issues around class are further complicated by the historical events of war and displacement. Upper-class families can become poor refugees overnight, as in my mother's case. Given this context, their silence could be viewed as conspiratorial. Perhaps it is the only given in an immigrant context — to strive to be middle- or upper-middle class — the American Dream. Perhaps it is the matrix in which all other experiences of race and gender are embedded. It seems to be a homogenizing force in the context of the differentiating force of racism. For these girls, identity formation during adolescence is not only a gender/sexual formation, but perhaps more profoundly, a racial formation embedded in the matrix of class. And racial-gender-class formation has spiritual dimensions, which is the theme of the next and final section.

I's Wide Shut

[Jane] is not doing this [eyelid surgery] because she wants to be "white," or because she's trying to erase her Asian-ness. But there is a sense that we are trying to erase something. What that is, is so much more complicated than our "slanty" eyes. I think we're trying to "erase" the feeling of shame and embarrassment, from all those kids that teased us growing up. Jane says that she always felt "vulnerable" because of her eyes, and I totally connect to that. I could buy all the designer clothes, cut my hair, wear the perfect pair of shoes, or hang out with the coolest people, but you can always get me on my "chinky" eyes.

—SuChin Pak from *My Life Translated 2*[29]

One common thread that seems to permeate the disparate experiences of these Korean American adolescent girls is a feeling of shame. Overtly or masked by other feelings, such as anger and bitterness, the feeling of shame seems to be a core in the identity formation of Korean American adolescent girls. Particularly if the shame is attached to a racial aspect of one's being, the racial formation of a person is embedded in the feeling of shame. Therefore, as SuChin Pak states so boldly and accurately, through eyelid surgery, or other "disciplinary" measures to "erase" our ethnic markers, we are trying to "erase" the feeling of shame. Shame and the effects of shame are a profoundly spiritual matter as it interferes with a "soul force energy" that demands an intimate relationship to God, oneself, and others.

In researching and writing this chapter, I struggled with my own spiritual ghosts that kept surfacing: ghosts of my own shame and how that affected my spirituality — my ability (or inability) and willingness (or unwillingness) to connect intimately with God and others. I struggled to differentiate between the eyelid surgery and other acts of marking the body permanently, e.g., tattooing and body piercing.

---

29. SuChin Pak, "SuChin's Journals," *My Life Translated 2*, *www.mtv.com/bands/m/mylifetranslated/index2.jhtml*, March 13, 2004.

In tattooing and body piercing, there is a sense of a positive claiming of one's body by carving out "a new paradigm" for one's self. It is a "conscientious, radical self-definition."[30] However, I struggled to see eyelid surgery in that same positive way. There is a qualitatively different feeling about the two acts. Only in writing this and struggling with my own ghosts did I realize that the difference is the feeling of shame. *Shame is what differentiates this act from adornment and makes it mutilation.* Perhaps shame is what makes Korean/Korean American mothers push their daughters to get eyelid surgery. They do not push for plastic surgery of other kinds — liposuction and breast augmentation, for instance.

Foucault was accurate in this: the power of the Gaze forces people to discipline themselves. Furthermore, it is interiorizing that Gaze that creates shame.[31] Shame is the force or the "internal eye/I" that drives a person to examine herself and then to discipline herself. This creates a spiritual dilemma. God, whom we know as all-knowing and all-seeing, also gazes upon us. If shame is the driving force for self-examination, is there room for God's gaze? What sort of self-examination does God's gaze bring about? How do we differentiate between shameful self-examination and healthy self-examination, e.g., "Examine yourselves to see whether you are living in the faith. Test yourselves. Do you not realize that Jesus Christ is in you?" (2 Cor. 13:5)? How do we foster spiritual formation that is not based on shame but on self-acceptance and freedom?

These are meta-questions that many adolescent girls struggle with. But Korean American adolescent girls experience "otherness" in ways that are particular to them and thus struggle with these questions in a

---

30. J. A. Silja, "Marked for Life: Tattoos and the Redefinition of Self," in *Body Outlaws,* 211–18.

31. Simone de Beauvoir articulates that adolescent girls' identity formation is based on shame. The biological function, namely, menstruation, which establishes a girl's identity, creates a sense of shame in our society, which has to deal secretly with menstrual flow and the sanitizing of the body. This creates a deep sense of shame in the formation of an adolescent girl's identity. *The Second Sex: The Classic Manifesto of the Liberated Woman* (New York: Alfred A. Knopf, 1952), 345–49.

particular way. And in their church context, they receive conflicting messages from the Bible and from their elders. They are taught that the Bible says that they are beautiful and good the way they are. But the women in the church and their critical gaze make them feel otherwise. The struggle to integrate and reconcile the different expectations of the ways one presents oneself before God (taking off the mask) and the ways one presents oneself before society — mother, family, school, friends — (putting on the mask) is in itself a task of adolescence as well as more generally a spiritual task.

Finally, I want to mention some perspectives that were not fully discussed in this chapter and ways they can foster further investigation and conversation: class, sexual orientation, and religious affiliation. The freedom to choose plastic surgery is a privilege of certain classes. Poor adolescent girls, no matter how much they wish to "self-discipline," cannot afford the $1,500–$3,000 to transform themselves. These Cinderellas, unless chosen to be a contestant on the *Swan* show,[32] will have to stay home and not go to the party. It would enhance this conversation to interview Korean American adolescent girls for whom such an expense is not an option. This raises further important questions: What are some of the ways *they* deal with the beauty myth? How do they "discipline" themselves to the Gaze? What are other feelings of shame associated with the poor working class? Which part of the identity formation — race, gender, or class — is their primary mode? What kind of masks do they wear?

Second, Korean American adolescent lesbians would respond to this quandary in another way. For adolescents coming to terms with their sexuality, their "difference" is marked outwardly by their body: how they look, how they sit and walk, and how they move. The complexity of this issue, which involves normative notions of femininity, dress,

---

32. The *Swan* show is a reality show that selects two "ugly" ducklings (women) and then transform them through plastic surgery, and speech, hair, and body work. During this time of transformation, these women do not have access to a mirror. They do not know, until the day of revelation in public, what they look like. One of them, then, is chosen to be in the Swan beauty contest.

and visual appearance, along with the notion of "butch-femme" roles, remains beyond the scope of this chapter. Nonetheless, it would be interesting to know what lesbian Korean American adolescents think of eyelid surgery. Are they more or less inclined to undergo it?

Another issue related to sexual orientation is the reality of the "closet" as a mask. Because of the ability, in some instances, to hide one's sexual identity, or at least attempt to "pass" as heterosexual, the closet is a complicated reality for lesbians. However, it is even more complicated for people of color who have to negotiate the juxtaposition of being "out" as a racial minority, but "in" as a sexual minority. This dynamic creates a paradoxical mask that is highly visible at the same time highly invisible.

Third, religion, either consciously or unconsciously, portrays normative images of women. It would be interesting to consider the differences between Korean American adolescent girls who are Christian and those who are Buddhist in relation to eyelid surgery. Do theologies that are informed by the concepts of new life, rebirth/being born again, transformation, and being a new creature foster and empower a need to physically re-create themselves? Do the theologies or religious belief systems affect these girls' sense of who they are visually?

In this chapter we have examined the relationship between "eyes" and "I's" for Korean American adolescent girls. This surgery has the potential to shut down the "I" while opening up the "eye." I have used eyelid surgery as a lens through which to look at the effect of racism and sexism on the spirituality and the identity formation of these girls. But the issue is larger than the eyelid surgery. As religious educators, we need to be attentive to ways in which we create masks for protection and what roles these masks play in spiritual formation. Perhaps masks are as inevitable and as human as scabs forming on a wound. And maybe, then, our task is to help one realize the existence of the mask and to help negotiate the "putting on" and "taking off" of the mask. This task we must do, with our "I's" wide open.

Chapter 2

Gods and Grandmothers

Spiritual Values of Resistance to Racism among African American Adolescent Girls

EVELYN L. PARKER

On Saturday, Grandma Vergie sternly reminded Clarence Powell, the drugstore clerk in Mt. Olive, Mississippi, that her name was Vergie not "gal."

On Sunday her straight back settled into the second pew of Mt. Pleasant C.M.E. Church. She uttered few Amens and Thank Jesuses, but her posture seemed to receive "life-giving" words and reject "fire and brimstone."

On Monday, she picked cucumbers at daybreak and supervised their delivery to be processed at the cucumber vat by mid-morning.

On Tuesday, she firmly pulled each teat of the cow until they filled the stainless-steel pail with milk just before her sisters, Amanda and Maud, arrived to stitch the new patchwork quilt.

On Wednesday, she fed the chickens, hogs, and cows early in the morning and then churned the milk into creamy, yellow butter.

On Thursday, she supervised the busload of hand hired to pick cotton while filling her own sack with the white commodity.

On Friday, she weeded the vegetable garden and gathered squash, okra, and butter beans.

On Saturday, Grandma Vergie reminded Miss Lucille, the store clerk at Calhoun's Mercantile in Mt. Olive, Mississippi, who she was, the eldest daughter of John and Effie McNair, and that Miss Lucille should watch how she spoke to her in the future.

Courageous, tenacious, audacious, bodacious: these adjectives describe the character of my grandmothers, my mother, and my mother's sisters. These women, Elizabeth my paternal grandmother, Vergie my maternal grandmother, her daughters, including my mother, Geraldine, and my aunt Juliet, are God's model of resistance against oppression. My childhood was formed in the midst of a racist, sexist, and classist milieu in the Southeast. Jim Crow was the reigning ideology of southern culture. I remember as a child wanting ice cream during a hot summer day while shopping in the small town of Mt. Olive, Mississippi. My parents would take me to the Dairy Dream for soft-served vanilla ice cream. They always reminded me that we would not be served at the front window if we stood in that line, that we had to go to the side window for service. I remember the uneasy feeling in the pit of my stomach as we did so. I also remember colored water fountains and bathrooms downtown as well as colored restaurants and funeral homes on the colored side of town that we affectionately called "the Quarters." Churches had either white or black congregations. In my world there was no alternative. The only distinction for the congregation of a church was between the black Methodists and the black Baptists.

Grandma Vergie taught me how to resist and defy racist white people. While shopping in Mt. Olive, where it seemed that everyone knew almost everyone else, I remember my grandmother was never cowed in the presence of white store clerks, white pharmacists, or white mill workers. First, we would drop the corn off at the mill for grinding. In crisp declarative tones she made her request known, that the corn should be ground into cornmeal for baking cornbread. Then we would walk to the general store where she would purchase needed items for our farm and home. At each stop Grandma Vergie's words would respectfully address white store clerks as well as black women and men from the community. They in turn would respectfully address her as "Miss Vergie." I don't ever recall white men or women calling her gal or mammy. Perhaps such events never happened in my presence. However, I do remember her eye-to-eye gaze, her erect posture, and the firm tone of her voice when she spoke to white women and men. Grandma Vergie was serious, never playful, with white folk.

When I was about six years old a white salesman came to talk with my aunt Maude at the "big house" where she lived. Aunt Maude, Grandma Vergie's sister, had inherited the enormous wood-frame house with its many large bedrooms, spacious hallway, kitchen, and dining area from their parents, Great Grandpa John and Great Grandma Effie. Aunt Maude lived "up the lane," about a quarter mile north of Grandma Vergie's farm. This white man's visit was regarding some matter that I didn't understand. I only remember it was important enough for my grandmother and mother to be there. They walked around the yard and talked for what seemed to a child like hours. The white man appeared friendly and comfortable in the presence of my family. At one point all the adults were standing in a circle talking and I was included in the circle, standing near the white man. Just as the conversation was tapering off he placed his hands on my shoulders affirmingly, like a family member would have done. Just as all others started to walk away he quickly pulled my small frame close to his body and moved his hands down to my pelvic area, outlining my "private part" with his large white hands. Somehow I pulled away and caught up with my mother. In a state of shock and fear, I was silent. My mother asked me what was wrong as the white man waved goodbye and drove off in his car. I told her what had happened to me. I will never forget her instructions. She said if any man, white or black, ever put his hands on me again I should immediately holler for her. I knew from her firm words that that white man would have never made it safely off our property if I had hollered for her help during his inappropriate touching. My mother, like Grandma Vergie, harbored no fear of white people. They elicited in them a fierce determination to defend their children, even unto death. Likewise, they modeled their fearless engagement of our Jim Crow world.

My grandmother, mother, and aunts taught me to defy the objectifying advances of white men and the dehumanizing directives of white women with a belief in God, through the power of the Holy Spirit, who wants me to flourish in this world. With a daring gaze, a stern voice, and heels dug in the ground, these women showed me how a black woman can survive and thrive in North America even amid its legacy of enslaving people from Africa.

Forty years hence grandmothers, mothers, and othermothers continue to be God's tangible grace for African American girls who struggle to survive amid forms of racism, sexism, and classism. Unlike the Jim Crow era in which I came of age, today racial oppression tends to be more subtle and tacit, although just as venomous. African American teenagers experience acts of racial profiling while shopping in malls or driving on city and suburban streets. Public school districts stream black teenagers disproportionately into special education classes or other less challenging non-college preparation curriculums. Henry Giroux, education and cultural studies professor, argues that "media culture is the central terrain on which the new racism has emerged. What counts as a source of education for many youth appears to reside in the spawning of electronic media, including radio talk shows, television, and film."[1] Giroux convincingly argues that the United States is at war with youth through its representation of them.

> How a society understands its youth is partly determined by how it represents them. Popular representations, in particular, constitute a cultural politics that shapes, mediates, and legitimates how adult society views youth and what it expects from them. Such representation, produced and distributed through the mass media in television, video, music, film, publishing, and theater, functions as a form of public pedagogy actively attempting to define youth

---

1. Henry A. Giroux, *Fugitive Cultures: Race, Violence, and Youth* (New York: Routledge, 1996), 58.

through the ideological filters of society that is increasingly hostile to young people. All of these sites make competing claims on youth and their relation to the social order. At worst, they construct youth in terms that largely serve to demonize, sexualize, or commodify them, to reduce their sense of agency to the consumerist requirements of supply and demand. Such images not only resonate with larger public discourses that contribute to a panic about youth, they also help to legitimize policies aimed at both containing and punishing young people, especially those who are marginalized by virtue of class, gender, race, and sexual orientation.[2]

African American girls struggle against the subtle assaults of race, class, and gender oppression as Giroux has argued, sometimes unaware of the source of the assault. Movies that represent black girls through racialized stereotypes are one cause of such struggle. The films *Bring It On* and *Bring It On II* are examples of racial stereotypes of black girls. In *Bring It On*, two opposing cheering squads, one from a predominately black high school in poor East Compton, California, the Clovers, and one from an upper-class suburban white neighborhood in San Diego, the Toros, prepare to compete against each other in a high stakes cheerleading championship. The "perfect" bodies, long hair, and narrow facial features of the cheerleaders from the black school represent the "beautiful" black teenage girl. Their white counterparts represent the physical ideal for white teenage girls: long blonde hair, blue eyes, and "buffed" bodies. After spying on the black cheerleaders, the former Toro captain steals the Clovers' choreography but claims the dance routine as her own. A series of confrontations is sparked by the Clovers' discovery that their dance routine has been stolen by the former white captain. The Toros' new captain hires a professional choreographer to teach the cheerleading squad a new dance routine, but the effort fails. In the meantime the Clovers' captain struggles to earn enough money to cover their travel expenses to the cheerleading

_____

2. Ibid., 110.

championship. With the pressure on, both captains drive their teams to exhaustion, each with different goals. The Toros' captain attempts to save her team's reputation and the Clovers' captain is determined to get the recognition that her team deserves. The Clovers' cheerleading squad wins the championship but this victory foreshadows the sequel, *Bring It On II*.

Analysis of the first movie gives us insight into how black and white girls are represented, particularly the black girls. While there is a clear subplot of competition between the sexualized bodies of both the black and white girls, the stereotypes of the black teenage females harken back to perceptions of black female slaves. Representing black teenage girls as sexualized bodies points to the stereotype of the highly sexual, nymphomaniac black woman created during the slave period in the United States. Such animal behaviors in black women justified the disdain, torture, and rape of female black bodies. Additionally, the black teenage girls are shown as lacking concern for educational achievement and social uplift. They are also stereotypically represented as having an "attitude," demonstrated in the neck swerving and finger-snapping gestures that allude to the mythical black superwoman who will fight anyone to defend her honor. Black teenage girls are also represented as concerned about their physical appearance and dancing provocatively in order to be chosen for the popular high school activity of the cheerleaders' squad. Likewise, they are stereotypically represented as being great dancers, worthy of their choreography being plagiarized — which again places an objectifying gaze on their physicality rather than affirming their intellectual and spiritual capacities. Seldom do such movies represent black teenage girls as connected to a larger matrix of family, church, and community. Rarely are the girls represented in wholesome relationships with mothers, grandmothers, and othermothers who model spiritual values that empower black girls to be suspicious and critical of racial and gender stereotypes that dehumanize them.

Spiritual values are embodied by those African American women who have "tried to move African Americans toward social equality through their religious traditions."[3] Many womanist scholars write of such spiritual values in various contexts. Among these scholars is Teresa Fry Brown, who extensively discusses the passing on of spiritual values of black grandmothers, mothers, and othermothers to their children. Citing black feminist Patricia Hill Collins, Brown describes the occasional pejorative definitions ascribed to grandmothers and othermothers by white dominant society that objectify black women and justify racism. Within the bonds of African American women spiritual values are passed on to black female children and adolescents. Brown writes:

> Mothers pass on everyday knowledge to their daughters for survival. Othermothers — aunts, grandmothers, sisters, cousins, neighbors, teachers — take on temporary or long-term child care or mentoring of younger women who are alone or whose blood mother is unable or chooses not to raise her children. These fluid boundaries reinforce the existence of the extended family through *fictive kin*.[4]

When faced with race, gender, and class oppression, how do black teenage girls respond? What is the relationship of their spirituality to their struggle against racism, sexism, and classism? How have significant women (mothers, grandmothers, aunts) raised the consciousness of their black daughters about subtle racial and gender assaults? What promise do the experiences of black teenage girls hold for the shaping of a wholesome spirituality? What might their experiences imply for the black community and the church?

This chapter shares the stories of five African American adolescent girls who, although they did not explicitly acknowledge it, learned from their mothers, grandmothers, godmothers, aunts, and othermothers to negotiate the troubles of race and gender while clinging to a caring God who offers "amazing grace" in the midst of difficult situations.

---

3. Teresa L. Fry Brown, *God Don't Like Ugly: African American Women Handing on Spiritual Values* (Nashville: Abingdon Press, 2000), 59.

4. Ibid., 60.

These girls, unaware of their attitudes of class elitism, express concerns to uplift other African American adolescents even as they unknowingly struggle with internalized classism and sexism regarding their own physicality.

To honor their anonymity as they shared their stories I asked the girls to choose pseudonyms. They choose Nicolé, Dell, Éve, Kay, and Mia. The first four girls are fifteen years old and sophomores; Mia is sixteen years old and a senior. All five girls are members of the middle class. They are all members of two-parent households; the parents' occupations include an accountant, an engineer, a college professor, and a public school teacher. In addition to secular jobs, some of the parents are also ordained ministers in Protestant denominations. Two of the young women are "PKs," or preachers' kids. Four of the girls are members of a Missionary Baptist church. Kay claims dual membership in both a United Methodist church and a Missionary Baptist church. They all attend church regularly, ranging from several times a week to a minimum of once a week. Their frequent church attendance reflects their involvement in various church activities and leadership roles. Éve and Dell serve as officers in their youth groups. All the girls attend worship and sing in the choir. All the girls except Kay attend Sunday school. Mia commented: "I am in just about everything that you can be in a church because my dad is pastor." Each girl was asked to describe her life through the metaphor of a song. This song could be one they have heard or one they compose. Nicolé, Dell, Éve, Kay, and Mia all graciously shared intricate aspects of their lives as young African American women.

"With the Lord on One Arm and Your Grandmother on the Other"

She was always humming. . . . Going to sleep with that warm sound clinging to your ears made fear impossible. You simply drifted off to the accompaniment of a murmured "Sleepin', Sleepin', Sleepin' in the arms of the Lord." . . . No matter what time she [Lutie Johnson] reached the house she knew in the back of her mind that Granny was there and it gave her a sense of security that Bub had never known.[5]

School is often a site of struggle against racial injustice for Nicolé, Dell, Éve, Kay, and Mia; they face racial insults from white peers as well as a racist wielding of power by white teachers. Acknowledging the presence of God and a grandmother or mother who cares, protects, and models tenacity helps a young black coed to negotiate the racist insults of a white teacher. The heading to this section is a quotation from Nicolé, who discussed a confrontation with a white teacher. She was somewhat reluctant to name as racist her conflict with the teacher. She did, however, indicate that the conflict was related to her being a young black woman. Nicolé's own words reveal the effort to examine all the possible causes for the conflict before naming it racist.

I have struggled with a teacher, and I thought it was because she was mean, because she was just mean to everyone else. And I mean, you say teachers are mean, but she was. And then I'm thinking, well I'm doing my best; this is all I can do. I'm asking questions, I'm coming to tutoring, and yet it seems like all these extra things I'm putting forward seems to be setting me back. I'm taking two steps, and it's knocking me back ten. And it, it even went so far as to making me fail one of our six-week sessions. That's how far it went. And I just, when I got that report card and saw that grade, I just couldn't do anything but beg the Lord to help me work with myself to figure out what it is that I'm doing wrong and figure out what to do. Should I go talk to this teacher? Should I have my parents talk to her to help me figure it out? I wasn't the only one in the class who was struggling, but I was the only one in the class who was failing. So I'm thinking, okay, I'm the only African American female in the class. . . .

---

5. Ann Petry, *The Street* (Boston: Houghton Mifflin, 1946), 404. This quotation is taken from a longer quotation in Fry Brown's *God Don't Like Ugly*, 79.

It was just two African American males and myself. And I'm thinking, well okay, she's not treating anyone else like this. I don't want to have a big race, racial thing blowing out of this, but it's like, okay, I'm trying. I don't know what else to do. I'm doing what you say, yes ma'am, no ma'am, I'm trying my hardest, okay can you help me a little bit. And I'm just putting all these feet forward and it's just like, you got to meet me half way on this. And the Lord blessed me in a way, well, I wouldn't say it was a blessing. But she had to go, and she didn't come back for the rest of the year. After that, my grades started pulling up and pulling up. And I was just like, "Lord, maybe that was the person that you needed to get out of my life. And I put it all in You, back to Philippians 4:13, I put it all in You." I said there is nothing else I can do, I gave it up. I mean, I had tried to figure it out myself, and that didn't work. So I put it in Him, and he fixed it for me. So that really renewed my faith, and it's just like He's there solving the problems for me and He's helping me along the way. I think some people have a problem with giving it all to Him. Some people give Him a little bit and then work on it a little bit more and then decide they need to give Him a little bit more once that stops working. And it takes them awhile to give it all. If you give it all in the beginning, He'll do it a lot faster instead of you give a little bit, take a little bit, give a little bit, take a little bit. You can't go back and forth with God. You gotta give it, or not give it.

In addition to explaining her conflict with the white teacher, Nicolé gives testimony of God's activity in her situation. She believes that God removed the teacher from her class, and with the new teacher she started to make passing grades. This testimony brought Nicolé full circle to a song she would write that gives witness to God's activity in her life. "I can do all things through him who strengthens me," she says, quoting Philippians 4:13. She also adds commentary on the rewards of "putting it in Him, and He fixed it for me." She cautions others not to vacillate between keeping part of their problem and giving a portion to God; she urges others to completely give their problems over to the Divine.

With further probing Nicolé revealed the conflict that emerged between her and the teacher.

> It's a thing that sometimes Caucasian people don't understand about how African American people express themselves. We're very emotional people. We express ourselves very flamboyant. We're out there, and we let people know that we're there. And there was this one situation she [the teacher] said I threw a fit, and it wasn't that I threw a fit. It was just that I was upset because my lunch had arrived late. My dad was supposed to bring it to me, and he got there late, and we weren't allowed to bring food in the library, but I had nowhere else to go. And she was like, tell her to throw her food away. And so I was like . . . she said, "Either throw your food away or leave!" And I'm like, "I'm not going to throw my food away. That's my parents' hard-earned money that I'm just gonna . . . he just bought it and I'm just gonna throw it in the trash. And I'm not going to be able to eat anything until I get home at like nine 9 o'clock because I had drill team practice after school. And I didn't have any money, so I wouldn't have been able to eat anything all day. This other girl, the next day, we were in the library and another girl brought her food in, and she didn't do anything, you know. And I was just like, well . . . she even wrote me up.

The conflict between Nicolé and the teacher resulted in a referral being written against Nicolé and an eventual parent-teacher conference before she could continue to attend class. Nicolé went on to say, "If you're gonna do something, have the Lord on one arm and your grandmother on the other and still do it, and not feel bad, then you're doing the right thing." She commented that it is important that a mother or grandmother be present during such confrontations.

She says that I threw a fit in her class, but I didn't. I just was like, "Well, I'm not gonna throw my food away." She said, "Well, you can leave." And I said, "I will leave." And I knew my parents were going to be behind me in my decision to leave. My mom said that if she would have made you throw your food away, it would have been a big problem. And I knew if I didn't go to class, it was the right thing, the Lord, and my parents and everybody would be behind me. Even if it is a racial issue, as long as you know that that is something you would do with the Lord on one arm and your grandmother on the other, then you know that you're doing the right thing.

Nicolé's detailed discussion of her experience with the white teacher and her response sanctioned by the presence of God and her grandmother sparked related discussions of struggle and the role of mothers. Ève talked about unconditional love and her white friends.

People change. One day they don't like you, the next they do. And it's just, like, I wish everyone could just love me just like God loves you. His love is unconditional, and like . . . seventh, eighth grade, I was having friend troubles. And I go to a majority white school. So two girls were my friends for a long time, then you know, they really don't want to hang around, invite me places and stuff like that, but they would talk to me and stuff at school.

Interviewer: Who were these girls? Were they African American girls? Describe them.

They were all Caucasian. My mom had kind of been trying to tell me that this was going to happen and you need to make other friends, because there were like four other African American girls that were coming into my grade. But you know, I didn't really know them because they were new. [Referring to the white girls] And so, I would talk to them and stuff. And around eighth grade I started realizing that, why am I talking to these people, wasting my time, just like following them around, doing stuff for them, and they're not even including me in any of their activities outside of school? God will always love you, so I know somebody will always care about me. And I know my parents care about me, but yeah . . . still knowing God will unconditionally love you.

Interviewer: God will?

Unconditionally love.

Nodding her head, Dell clearly agreed with Éve. So I invited Dell to comment on unconditional love. Her comments open up the question of mothers as omniscient, at least when it comes to knowing about relationships that cross the boundaries of race and ethnicity as well as those within the African American community.

The reason why I was agreeing with her is because my mom is always like, "They're not your friends. You have to watch out for them." People have really used me in that sort of way, so I know what she's talking about. I had a life-changing, new experience. Long story short, I was hanging out with a group of girls, and they were talking about one of the girls. All the girls were African American, even though I went to a predominately Caucasian school at one point. And I hung out with them a lot and everything, and basically, they were talking about this one girl, and she was not new, but she had got held back or whatever. And she kind of bossed people around because she thought she was older and wiser, and they would talk about her. Then one day, I just got tired of her, and I kind of stood up to her. No one, none of them, they didn't stand behind me. They just said, "I'm not in it, I'm not in it." I'm looking around the table and I'm like, "You guys, are you serious? You were just talking about her like five minutes ago." And they're like, "I'm not in," and I realized at that moment, sixth grade, I'm like twelve. I'm like, oh my goodness, I can't believe that this happened. My mom said it was going to happen and it did. And I just basically disowned myself from them and I went and sat at another table. And they all pretty much came back to me in the end. And we're friends to this day, but I'll never forget what they did to me.

Dell's story led to vibrant conversation about mothers among the girls. Kay commented: "Don't you just hate it when the mothers are right?" All the girls laughed as they said "Yeah." Kay continued:

It's just that they say something over and over again, and you're just like, "Don't tell me that again." And then when it happens. ...Mothers are always right. Always, always....

Interviewer: Oh, always?

Kay: Always! Always! Yes, always right! She knows everything. No, no, no...she doesn't know everything, but she knows when things like that are going to happen, like friends, school situations, and she's always right. She probably went through lots of it herself though. That's what I was thinking.

Kay refers to Dell:

You probably have more of the same personality than you know. That's what I can't stand about my mom. She and I have some things that are similar, but I'm more athletic and she's more academic. She just knows me all too well and I can't stand it. I can't say in too much detail, but you know how they say stuff over again. You're like, "Okay, you don't know me. I'm my own person" and then you do it, and you're like, "Don't tell Mom." And then they always know. They always know. And then they're like, "It happened, didn't it?" And you're like, "I don't know what you're talking about."

The lively interchange about all-knowing mothers tapered off. The discussion transitioned to other experiences of racial and gender oppression. Mia, a very reserved senior, entered the conversation speaking of her autobiographical song, her struggles with race, and the hopes she holds for her offspring.

I can think of something that happened about, I guess it was February. Something that happened when we went back to school after the Christmas break. And I did this UIL thing, we had UIL competitions on Saturdays.

Interviewer: What is UIL?

University Interscholastic League, but this was an academic one so we had to be at school at 6:30 in the morning. And so, you got there for probably like eight hours but you only compete for an hour and just sit around for the rest of the time. So we sat there and we were talking and stuff about, I don't know.... And one was Catholic, none of them was black, and one was Afghani. And he was talking about how he couldn't be president and stuff. One guy was talking about being president and the Afghani guy was like, "I can't be president because I wasn't born here." And I was thinking, "You know, I was born here and I still can't be president...." The song makes me think that, you know, maybe one day in my life, or maybe not in my life but my family's or something like that, maybe like my kids or my grandkids or something like that, you know, this country will get to a point where when you first see somebody they won't ask, you know, what color is she or what color is he, or is it a boy. They won't ask that question. It's, you know, what does that person do. My song makes you think that maybe not now, but wait.

Mia hopes for a future where color and gender will not matter, even to be elected as president of the United States.

Kay chimed in with experiences of racial oppression in high school. The passion in her voice and the repetition of horrific details bears witness to her egregious ninth-grade year.

I'm from California so I'm not used to ... like for the first time I was called a light-skinned black person and I was like, "I'm still black, you know." I never really had that problem with California, and then I came to Texas and then it was black, white, and

Mexican. And then I went to Southland Hills [a pseudonym], and it was predominantly white and they didn't accept any culture, nothing, unless it was like Italian, but it had to be white. And that was even too much for them because they were dark white people. So if they can't even accept the Italians, you can imagine what it was like for me coming in, a person of color, and then they didn't accept that I was a pre-AP student [Advanced Placement]. They didn't accept that I played basketball. Well, they were like, "Oh, she's black. Of course she plays basketball." Like with basketball, they were like, all black kids play sports. That's how they thought of me, and I could tell just by the way they would respond. Like when I was hurt, with the white people, they would let them take breaks, but with me, it was like, "You can do it! Black people are stronger." And I'm like, I'm a human, I need a break. It hurts. And they just wouldn't accept. Math has always been my best subject, and I got sick earlier in the year and I missed a week or two, which is very bad to start off at the beginning of the year. When you're sick, you're sick. You can't stop it. And so I came back, and I did well on all of my tests and stuff, and I ended up with a 74. And I was confused. I was like, "How can I do well and end up with a 74?" I went to my counselor, but she was also racist. I went to my principal; he was also racist. So I was like, okay, what can I do? I went to my mom and dad. They were like, I don't care how smart you are, you're black. And so they [the school officials] wouldn't listen to that, and they would just put me in a state like all black people suck. I would get into a state where I hated white people, and I wanted to beat them up. Before, I was like, there are some racist white people and there are some that are liberal and date black people, date Mexicans, they don't care. But with me, I just hate white people. Even if a white person looks at me funny, they could be my friend, since I've been through all this, since I didn't have a lot of friends. Because I was at the bottom, because I was middle class and I was black. Even the middle-class white people didn't accept me. Just because they're white, they have something over me. So I was like, what am I going to do?

There was this one girl, I'll never forget her name, Janice Adkins [pseudonym]. She would take me out to places too. She was the only person, and all her other friends would be like, "Are you sure?" I heard them. They thought I couldn't hear. I don't know. They thought I was so dumb I couldn't hear, but you know, they would be like, "Are you sure you want her to come? I mean, other people will stare." I was like, you know, I just want to have fun.

Other people have seen black people and associate with them. It's not a great big shock.

[The girls laughed.]

They act like it's the 1960s or something.

Yeah, Southland Hills is stuck in the 1960s so people . . . they'd be like, well, were the academics too hard? I'd be like, you know, it was easy. It was that they were stuck in the 1960s. They say they have the smartest education, but you don't have the best education until you know about other cultures and learn to accept them. Then you are intelligent. Like, for me, I used to know Koreans, but now I've been away from California too long.

At this point in the interview I asked the other girls if they had had experiences similar to Kay's. Again Mia was the first to reply.

Well, I can relate because I live in Kerryfield [a pseudonym] and that was the last district in Texas to integrate. So we are still kind of stuck there. I don't too much get stares because I've seen these people all my life. But they'll say things like, "You're pretty articulate for a black girl." So are you insinuating that the majority of black people are dumb? And they're like, "No, you're smart." And they'll say things like that.

And the reason our district integrated at all was for a football player coming, so it was for the athletics. It's just as far as me being smart, . . . I was working on my schedule when I was in the eighth grade. I was gonna go to high school. I was all excited.

And my counselor, she was like, "You know you got four pre-AP classes?" And I was like, "Well, yeah, I am taking four core classes so that makes sense." She was just like, "Well, don't you think that's just gonna be a little too hard for you?"

Kay: That's what they did with me too.

Mia: And I was like, "No, it's not gonna be too hard for me." And then you get those things like, "Maybe that's not the right class for you." It's almost like honest ignorance. They'll say it, but they don't mean anything.

Interviewer: Honest ignorance?

Yeah, they're not trying to be mean at all. They'll be like, "You're doing good for a black kid" and they don't even realize what they just said. And it's like, "Do you realize what you said?" And they don't know. It's just like, "Well, why are you offended?" I've had kids say, "Black people should be able to get jobs and go to school and stuff." And they'll just sit there and say something like that, and it's just so ignorant, and they don't even realize they said it. They don't understand what you're mad about, what you're offended for.

It was evident that Mia and Kay had battle scars from bouts of racism with their schoolteachers, administrators, and peers. Although recalling their experiences reminded them of the mental and even physical pain they endured, these girls recounted the spiritual values of perseverance and hope as instrumental in helping them combat the racial oppression they experienced.

The Amazing Grace of Othermothers

The girls' playful reflections on omniscient mothers connected with Dell's life story, which she had shared earlier in the interview session. Without any hesitation Dell stated that her autobiographical song was

"Amazing Grace" and followed up with an explanation of its relevance to her life.

I chose an old song. I chose "Amazing Grace." It has to do more with my first mom and things that happened when I was younger that I didn't really have control over. It' just because I think amazing grace got me to where I am now and my parents and everything. My mom got pregnant with my older sister when she was a sophomore in college, and later she decided she wanted to go back to school to continue on with her education, so she left her with my grandparents. She went back, and about a year and a half later she got pregnant with me, and she still wanted to continue on with her education and go back to college and everything so she made a deal . . . actually, not a deal. She decided to talk to my aunt, and she and my uncle decided to take care of me so she could finish college and come back and take care of us on her own. And like, when I was two, I had lived with them for two years, and my aunt and uncle were like, you don't have a job, you don't have a place to live, how are you going to take care of two kids by yourself? And she had my brother, like, she was pregnant with my brother also. So I think, it' just like amazing grace that helped me get where I am now because the parents I have now provided a better life than she could ever imagined for me to have. You know, they sent me to good schools. They sent me to private schools. I was raised as an only child. I wasn't a middle child. I had the things that only children have, you know . . . the spoilage and everything. So, I think it was just kind of meant by God's grace for me to be with them, you know. It just kind of turned out that way, and it wasn't kind of like necessarily meant for it to happen that way.

Interviewer: So your parents are actually your relatives?

Yeah. My mom is actually my real mother's aunt . . . She's my great-aunt. So it's my Great-Aunt Sarah [pseudonym].

Clearly Dell embraced her great-aunt and uncle as her "true" parents. This acknowledgement obviously illustrates the place of othermothers in the nurturing of black daughters as reflected in the earlier quote from Teresa Fry Brown (see p. 49) and the writings of many black feminist and womanist scholars. Although the circumstances vary among adopted black "baby girls," there is usually an aunt, an othermother, who claims the child as her own. Rita Dove writes about aunts in black women's literature: "Though aunts are often significant people in extended families — especially in black families — they tend to be represented in literature as childless, marginal figures."[6] Whether childless, widowed, or divorced, aunts have played a significant role as othermothers in the lives of black children.

In her autobiography Pauli Murray writes endearingly about her Aunt Pauline. She adopted three-year-old Pauli after strong admonitions from family and friends that a girl child offered nothing but heartaches and troubles. Aunt Pauline made the decision to adopt her namesake after the death of her sister, Pauli's mother, and Pauli's father's mental illness. Pauli's description of her Aunt Pauline gives a glimpse of the highly revered character her aunt embodied and Pauli no doubt emulated. Each Sunday Aunt Pauline attended church twice: "morning service at her own Saint Titus Episcopal Church and evening service at the neighborhood Second Baptist Church, which many of her students and their parents attended."[7] Teaching, for her, was the act of "building character, molding and shaping the future"[8] rather than simply conveying knowledge. "Whether a child was pliable and responsive or wooden and inflexible, she sensed the possibilities. She envisioned the finished product, the fine grain of wood beneath a rough and splintered exterior."[9] Aunt Pauline was strict, demanding accuracy and precision and full ownership of one's responsibilities. She blended

---

6. May Helen Washington, ed., *Memory of Kin: Stories about Family by Black Writers* (New York: Anchor Books/Doubleday, 1991), 369.

7. Pauli Murray, *Pauli Murray: The Autobiography of a Black Activist, Feminist, Lawyer, Priest, and Poet* (Knoxville: University of Tennessee Press, 1987), 15.

8. Ibid., 16.

9. Ibid.

firm discipline and freedom to make one's own "choices and live with the consequences, however bizarre some of them might be."[10] Pauli writes:

> Aunt Pauline also took me back and forth with her to night school. Her adult pupils had never had an opportunity to learn to read and write. I became her small apprentice, and she kept me happily occupied erasing the blackboard, cleaning erasers, handing out copybooks, and sometimes even helping her elderly students with their lessons.[11]

Aunt Pauline was industrious, raised with her four other sisters and one brother to do whatever work was needed to maintain personal and familial independence. She was a farmer and a seamstress as well as a teacher. Concluding her chapter simply titled "Aunt Pauline," Pauli wrote: "On Mother's Day, when people wore flowers in tribute to their mothers, I could not decide whether to wear a white flower in memory of my real mother, Agnes, or a red flower in recognition of Aunt Pauline. It was characteristic of my way of resolving dilemmas that I wore both."[12] Pauli's Aunt Pauline symbolizes the nurturing yet powerful othermother who has historically shaped the character of black daughters. I do not intend to draw close parallels between Pauli's Aunt Pauline and Dell's mother, Great-Aunt Sarah, as women who embodied and apprenticed their daughters in spiritual values. However, given the nature of the relationships between black mothers and their daughters it is safe to conclude that Dell was apprenticed in her othermother's spiritual values just as Pauli was apprenticed in her Aunt Pauline's spiritual values. Grandmothers, mothers, and othermothers in the black community continue to teach their children practices of spiritual values.

---

10. Ibid., 26.
11. Ibid., 18.
12. Ibid., 27.

Trailer Park White People and
Ghetto Black People

When I invited the other girls to share their experiences of racial injustice, Nicolé spoke up. Her first statement suggested an experience similar to Mia's. "Yes, I have the whole thing with the 'You talk like a white person.'" However, her subsequent remarks indicated that such racial slurs as "You talk like a white person" were the fault of African American people. She stated:

> African American people won't take the time to educate them-
> selves. If we all took the time to educate ourselves, then we
> wouldn't feel bad when white people are like, "You are articulate
> for a black person." Once all black people start talking like that,
> then you can say, "Well, what are you comparing me to because
> all black people talk like this."

As Nicolé continued with a long and passionate discourse on educating blacks to talk appropriately, also arguing that uneducated whites talk inappropriately, she stated, "Trailer park white people are the same as black people who live in ghettos, same as black people who live in bad parts of town." Nicolé offered a class critique in which she appeared to believe that the troubles of poor people, "ghetto and trailer park" people, are rooted in their lack of education.

Kay agreed with Nicolé as she prescribed a solution for "ghetto blacks and trailer park whites." Kay discussed her intentional way of teaching inarticulate black students at her school how to talk appropriately.

> Some people say, "Why you use such big words?" They're not
> big words. I understand what they mean. I don't like it when
> people use words, and they don't be using them right. Then I
> correct them, and they get all mad. You ain't using a word right,
> even if I was...black, white, Mexican, whatever. You using a
> word wrong. I don't care what you are. If you use a word and it's
> wrong, I'm going to tell you...I grew up..., "Oh yeah, you're

acting white" kind of thing. So it just went through and I'm not going to change, turn around and be like, "Yo, yo, yo...start talking all ignorant."

Kay continued with a stream of comments about whites as the cause of black problems, the problem with black males, and black stereotypes. She then returned to describing her strategy of educating black students to speak properly. She also offered a critique of young black males using "the man" as "a scapegoat for laziness."

> Some people act their stereotype. With me, I learned that...I'm kind of like...I use education with slang at school, but it's like so mixed that they don't even catch it. So they actually learn vocabulary without knowing it, so I'm kind of bringing them toward the educated side.
>
> They don't know it, but then by the end of the year, they'll be speaking more articulate with the bigger words and then their moms are like, "You've been hanging around with that Kay too much!" And they get mad because they're speaking bigger words now. And so what I do is I take part of their stereotypical culture and I take my educated culture and I mix it so they feel comfortable talking to me and they learn at the same time. And that's what you really had to do. You have to kind of mix it, but don't go around like she said, "yo, yo, yo, what's up, what' the dealy-o" and all that stuff. No, no please don't do that. Don't do that. Mix it in so that they're comfortable and then teach them these words without them knowing. Just talk to them in big words and then they're going to ask you, "What does that mean?" And then they'll slowly start.

Kay and Nicolé's comments provide insights into the class struggle among black teenagers. Clearly they fail to recognize their own class biases and elitist attitudes.

While Mia, Dell, and Éve did not join the above conversation, Dell did express her fear of being discriminated against, an experience she has never had. Evidence of class strife among African Americans is apparent in her description of being told by other blacks that she's acting white.

> But yeah, it's mostly discrimination from people of my race. That's the only discrimination that I've really seen. I mean, we laugh and joke about it. It's funny. "Oh, you're acting white." It really does upset me, because I was raised with those type of people and I don't know any other way to act. I act...I'm me. And I don't act a certain way to please people. I'm me. And it really upsets me when they say, "Oh, you're talking white" or, "You're acting white."

As the girls' conversation moved toward their beliefs about what it means to live a meaningful life, they talked a lot about having material possessions, the importance of education beyond high school, and creating jobs for other people as business owners. In the midst of this vibrant conversation Mia spoke up.

> Well like, I don't need anything. Like I have a car...I don't need anything, but still I'm not happy. Apparently, all these worldly possessions and things aren't adequate, you know. You need stuff and you're not going to be happy if you've got a bill and you can't pay it. But you also need to have good relationships with people and things like that. You need to have other things. You don't just need like education...you need education, you need to go to college. You need to get whatever or make sure you're stable, but you need more than that because that's not all of it. I know my parents are going to pay for me to go to college. I know that if I were not to have a job and I were kicked out of my apartment or something like that that I could always come back to my parents, and I'll always know that I have that. But I'm not going to be necessarily happy with this and so apparently, I'm like, stuff doesn't do it all.

At this point both Dell and Kay recalled discussing the ingredients of having a balanced life, that well-being consisted of "leveling four parts: the intellectual, the emotional, the mental, and the physical." They concluded that perhaps Mia was going through a difficult time with the "emotional thing." Perhaps their unprofessional psychoanalysis is accurate. Even more interesting is the juxtaposition of Mia's critique that "having stuff" does not produce happiness with the other girls' concern for "having stuff." The girls' conversation raises questions about internalized classism among black teenagers.

Although a few scholars have offered theories on this phenomenon in African American teenagers, more scholarship is needed in this area. Marcia Riggs gives insight on internalized classism among blacks through her helpful discussion of social stratification among blacks in her book *Awake, Arise, and Act.* Riggs is concerned to offer "a mediating ethic for black liberation with intragroup social responsibility as its core value."[13] She develops this thesis by first offering in-depth discourse on social stratification as influenced by the wider North American society and within the black community. She argues that "the structures of social inequality operative in the society is the *constitutive* factor in the oppression of Blacks — an external dimension — whereas social stratification within the black community is a *derivative* factor — an internal dimension — that impedes black liberation."[14] Riggs offers a thorough analysis of the historical nature of social stratification within the black community, beginning with the nineteenth century and the enslaved black population up through the early twentieth century with W. E. B. Du Bois's "Talented Tenth." Social stratification among blacks includes economic, moral, political, and ideological dimensions. She offers the black women's club movement as an example of a liberative moral vision for the black community and the church for the twenty-first century. Riggs's argument

---

13. Marcia Y. Riggs, *Awake, Arise, and Act: A Womanist Call for Black Liberation* (Cleveland: Pilgrim Press, 1994), 5.

14. Ibid., 9.

is fundamental to understanding the problem of internalized classism among black teenagers.

It's Just Like a Circle

As the interview with Mia, Kay, Dell, Éve, and Nicolé moved to a close Nicolé talked about the role her mother played in giving her "stuff." Her reflections included the struggles her family members had while acquiring their material possessions. She said, "Like my great grandmother, she's still here. Even now, she instills stuff [beliefs] in me. And she passed it down to my grandmother, and my grandmother to my mom, and back to me. And it's just like a circle...I can look this way and be like, you know what, they did good."

Her audible stream of consciousness provides an interesting return to the questions posed earlier in this chapter and other related questions. When faced with race, gender, and class oppression how do black teenage girls respond? What is the relationship of their spirituality to their struggle against racism, sexism, and classism? How can they defy objectifying gazes and misogynistic naming of their person? How have significant women (mothers, grandmothers, aunts) subtly or overtly raised the consciousness of their black daughters about racial and gender assaults? What promise do the experiences of black teenage girls hold for the shaping of a wholesome spirituality? What might their experiences imply for the black community and the church?

Although the experiences of the above five African American female adolescents cannot be generalized to all middle-class black females, their stories demonstrate that grandmothers, mothers, and othermothers play a significant role in shaping their spiritual values. The practice of perseverance was a motif in all the girls' stories. Other practices of resistance that derive from their spiritual values are not readily discernable, however, which suggests the need for further probing and analysis of their stories. Perhaps I missed an opportunity by not pursuing such investigation. Nonetheless, I did find that the spiritual lives of these five black teenage girls are deeply influenced by grand-mothers, mothers, and othermothers. Both generations, like other black mothers and daughters, continue to struggle with the realities of being female and black in a world that continues to be patriarchal, sexist, misogynistic, and, as Du Bois has argued, where "the color line" continues to be a problem.

In light of the realities of racism, sexism, and classism, if the church — in which women and girls have long been the majority — is to be a relevant institution, then the church must discern ways to let girls tell their stories and receive God's miraculous healing in the process.

Chapter 3

From "Wanton Girle" to the Woman Who Fell from the Sky

The Sacred Selves of Native American Girls

LAURA E. DONALDSON

Broken Circles

I come from a long line of Cherokee Methodists and know firsthand the great spiritual strengths and creative cultural innovations of that particular variation upon Christianity. When federal authorities attempted to detribalize us by banning our language, criminalizing our religious ceremonies, and dividing collectively held ancestral lands into individual 160-acre plots, the Cherokee churches — both Methodist and Baptist — were one of the few institutions that actually nurtured the speaking of Cherokee and preserved traditional forms of tribal leadership. And Methodist and Baptist churches preserved traditional leadership models after the Cherokee Nation officially adopted an Anglicized governance model. However, my ancestors also include a group of Cherokees influenced by the Shawnee prophet Tenskwatawa and led by a controversial figure named Dragging Canoe. The so-called Chickamaugas — named for their northern Georgia and southern Tennessee homelands — violently opposed the physical and cultural encroachments of Anglo-America and, most especially, Christianity. After the failure of their armed rebellion, many left northern Georgia for Arkansas with the intent of constructing another Cherokee Nation far from white "civilization." I have struggled with this contradictory heritage for much of my childhood and adult life.

The Seneca girls interviewed for this anthology also speak of lives driven by contradiction. They are Native by descent but not recognized by their communities, living off the reservation but still yearning for acceptance and, most important, longing for spiritual wholeness but deprived of the cultural means to attain it. I was profoundly moved by the hard realities of their lives and their struggles to attain a sense of themselves, to claim their identity. I offer snippets of their stories in light of the contradictions that hinder their spiritual flowering. I will then honor these girls by reflecting on both the history and traditions by which Native girls have become women. I offer Pocahontas, who is surely the most famous Native woman in North America, as a fitting exemplar.

Visiting Handsome Lake's Daughters

On a Sunday afternoon in early August 2003, just after the upstate New York blackout, four teenage girls gave one-on-one interviews at the Four Corners United Methodist Church. The church is located on the Seneca Reservation about twenty-five miles south of Buffalo, New York. The interviewer had told the girls about this book and invited them to share their stories in the volume.[1] They came at the appointed time and waited patiently in the sanctuary of the church until it was their turn to talk with the interviewer. One by one they filed into the fellowship hall to sit at a small round table to share their life stories. Each girl chose a pseudonym to protect her identity. They chose Alexis, Molley, Mercedes, and Jayde. All the girls were historically connected to the reservation even though they may not have actually lived on the reservation. Only two of the girls actually lived there.

---

1. Cynthia Abrams conducted the interview with the four girls from the Seneca Nation. She is Seneca and has ties to the reservation and Four Corners United Methodist Church.

The Seneca Tribe is one of the five nations of the Iroquois Confederacy established in the late 1700s. They lived primarily in present-day western New York state and eastern Ohio. They were the largest and one of the most important members of the Iroquois Confederacy. Seneca women played a major role in the community as farmers and community organizers, especially during the men's hunting periods. Families, linked by maternal kinship, lived in longhouses. These dwellings not only provided shelter but eventually became traditional houses of prayer.[2]

A Seneca chief named Ganioda'yo, which means "Handsome Lake," founded the Longhouse religion in 1799 after receiving a vision from heaven. From this experience he transformed himself and the Seneca Nation. He adopted Christian beliefs, primarily from Quaker contacts. Jesus was revered as a local mythological figure. "Seneca rituals were modified to four transformed dance feasts and the longhouse was modified into a 'church.'"[3] Handsome Lake's teachings were embraced among the Iroquois and are still practiced today in various longhouses on Iroquois reservations in New York and parts of Canada.

While neither the girls nor the interviewer ever discussed the legacy of Handsome Lake, longhouses, or maternal influences on Seneca Native Americans, these historical tidbits provide a context for the life stories of Alexis, Molley, Mercedes, and Jayde. All the girls talked of struggles for acceptance and prejudice among those outside the community as well as within. Here I lift up Alexis's and Molley's stories because they reveal lives of contradiction and struggle for acceptance while living with and loving those on the brink of despair.

Broken Circle II

Alexis and her family are members of the Church of Jesus Christ of Latter-day Saints, the Mormons. They recently moved back to the

---

2. See "Seneca" at *Britannica Online: www.britannica.com.*
3. See "Handsome Lake Cult" at *Britannica Online: www.britannica.com.*

reservation after her father retired and joined a small Mormon church where almost everyone is related. Having lots of relatives in the same congregation has been a point of contention for Alexis. In contrast to her current faith community, she has fond memories of the large Mormon congregation just outside of Washington, D.C., which she attended for the first fifteen years of her life.

> I developed really good relationships with some of the people at my other ward, as we call it. And it was very diverse. I have Asian friends, Caucasian, African Americans, like everybody went to that church. It was just mixed. I developed my best friends in that ward. And I guess that's the biggest thing that I miss is that interaction with the youth there.

Alexis enjoyed being a member of the racially diverse youth group of her former ward. She found the youth leaders especially supportive. In contrast, she struggles at getting to know her relatives and to appreciate her heritage at her current ward.

> At first I hated it. I was a brat. I did not want to be here, but in all reality this is my true home, my roots. My parents are born and raised here, so I feel a bit more connected now that I'm comfortable. I actually have a hard time going back home sometimes. I do like it around here but, I don't know, I just feel more connected now that I know people, and now I can go to church and see them at the [fair] and I feel comfortable talking to them. And actually getting to know my relatives a little bit more but, I don't know.

Alexis practices the spiritual discipline of prayer when faced with temptations and is confronted with challenges. When asked about her coping method she replied:

> Prayer, lots of prayers. It doesn't even have to be on your knees or anything like that. It can just be a silent prayer when you

need the extra help, you need the extra boost. No, it can be at any time.

Although Alexis has roots in the Seneca community, these historical ties have not afforded her acceptance among her female peers. While some Native American males have befriended her, girls have not afforded her the same acceptance. She laments:

> In all honesty, I don't talk to girls from the reservation. I have a couple friends; they are my cousins. I'm considered...they call me a white girl. They say I'm an apple. I'm red on the outside, white on the inside. It's just I don't click with them.

Interviewer: Why do you think they say that?

Just because they are not used to me. They haven't given me the opportunity to hang out with them because they don't see me partying on the reservation. And I'm not doing things I shouldn't be doing. They don't see that so they think that I'm probably better than them. And it has a lot to do with their background. We had a talk with them, and we were like, "Why don't you like me?" They were just like, "We just don't. You're white. Your parents act like they're white." And I was like, "Well, what bothers you so much about me?" They're like, "Well, you live in a nice house, you have this, you have that, you have a car, you have a white boyfriend." And I said, "What really bothers you?" She was like, "Well, I go home and when I see my mom drunk, I see this, I see that." It's just they don't know any better in a way. And I was like, "Well, you don't have to take it out on me. I'm here to be your friend. We're like sisters in a sense. I know exactly what you are. We are a part of each other. Why destroy a connection like that?" They're like, "What are you talking about? You know nothing about me. You don't know how I have to go to bed every night. You don't know that my dad beats my mom." And I think it just has a big impact on them. They don't mean to be like that, it's just they see it that way. And I tell myself,

"Don't' hold it against them. Don't hold it against them. Don't have hard feelings toward these people because they just didn't have the life that I have or had growing up."

Broken Circle III

Molley is in the eleventh grade and lives in a small town near the reservation, where she attends First United Methodist Church. She is biracial: her father is Native American and her mother is European American. She does not recall bad experiences from racial prejudice but is aware of the tensions between those from the reservation and those who are not. When asked about her affiliations with girls from the reservation she replied:

No, I don't know, sometimes I kind of think that I'm not really accepted, just because I don't really know ... we don't have the same living situation, the same, you know, just neighborhoods or anything like that.

With a few probing questions Molley talks about her friend from the reservation but clarifies the degree to which she is Native American:

Actually my friend, she lives on the reservation, but everybody just sees her as being white because her mom is like an eighth or sixteenth or something. But you know, she rides the bus to school and stuff, and I guess, I don't know if that counts or not.

Molley, unaware of the implications of her statement, introduces the element of class while discussing her friend from the reservation. From that point on class matters thread throughout Molley's conversation. She is very concerned about the stereotypes given to Indians from the reservation. They are labeled as lazy, unwilling to work, and as having the land but never being willing to work for a better life off the reservation. Molley indicates that these erroneous beliefs held by prejudiced people are wrong and hurt those who have achieved academically. She recalls:

My mom ... well, she's close to some of my dad's cousins and sisters. So one of my aunts came by and she was talking about her daughter, how people, even though she's really smart and she went to a good college and everything, people are still like, from high school, "Oh, she's so perfect, but she's just an Indian."

Molley believes that teenagers make the stereotypes realities because there is little or no encouragement from teachers and administrators in the area schools. Even when students from the reservation are academically and professionally successful they are viewed negatively.

Molley and Alexis, like Mercedes and Jayde, long for unconditional acceptance in the community of their heritage. They embody the pain of the broken circle where their ancestors once danced. They long for the "spirit/Spirit" that offers them wholeness.

The "Wanton Girle"

Their younger women goe not shadowed amongst their owne companie until they be nigh eleaven or twelve returnes of the leafe old ... nor are they much ashamed thereof, and therefore would the before remembered Pochahuntas, a well featured but wanton young girle, Powhatan's daughter, sometymes resorting to our Forte, of the age then of eleven, or twelve, yeares, gett the boyes forth with her into the market place, and make them wheele, falling on their hands, turning their heeles upward, whome she would followe, and wheele so her selfe, naked as she was, all the forte over; but being once twelve yeares, they put on a kind of semecinctum lethern apron (as doe our artificers or handycrafts men) before their bellies and are very shamefac't to be seene bare.[4]

Not long after saving John Smith, a young daughter of Powhatan visited the fledgling settlement now known as Jamestown.[5] The girl's

---

4. William Strachey, *A Historie of Travaile into Virginia Britannia* (London: Hakluyt Society, 1849), 65.

5. Pocahontas belonged to the Pamunkey branch of the Powhatan confederacy.

revealing physicality when turning cartwheels around the fort shocked the British colonists, who criticized the behavior of "Pochahuntas" as frankly exhibitionist. Indeed, this incident was so vividly described by the colonial historian William Strachey that it was not published until 1849 — 237 years after its original recording. According to seventeenth-century British proprieties, girls should not freely associate with boys, much less cavort with them in a way that exposed their "privities."[6] In the pre-contact world of the Algonquian, however, prepubescent girls had few constraints on their activities and were only restricted after the onset of menstruation — a transition that Strachey confuses with chronology ("being once twelve yeares"). He also conflates Algonquian women's strong sense of modesty ("they...are very shamefac't to be seene bare") with a Christianized shame over the realities of the female body. Ironically, Strachey includes an Algonquian glossary in his "historie" of Virginia Britannia that belies his interpretation of Pocahontas's conduct. The Algonquian term for girl is *usqwasenis oc* — the root *sqwa* denotes a female and is the probable origin of the Euro-American word "squaw" — while *cutssenepo* denotes a sexually mature woman and *tumpseis,* a post-menopausal woman. These linguistic divisions turn on women's capacity or incapacity for reproduction with the interesting implication that they possess a different identity after the cessation of their childbearing years. Notably absent, however, is any term for adolescence — an absence revealing both the cultural and historical specificity of the present volume.

The concept of adolescence is a recent revision of the human developmental process, and its applicability to many indigenous cultures remains problematic. For example, a popular Internet resource on children's health in adolescence cautions parents that adolescence is not identical to puberty:

> Most of us think of puberty as the development of adult sexual characteristics: breasts, menstrual periods, pubic hair, and

---

6. Before the onset of menstruation, Algonquian girls wore only a moss thong over the genital area.

facial hair. These are certainly the most visible signs of impending adulthood, but children between the ages of 10 and 14 (or even younger) can also be going through a bunch of changes that aren't readily seen from the outside. These are the changes of adolescence. Many kids announce the onset of adolescence with a dramatic change in behavior around their parents. They're starting to separate from Mom and Dad and to become more independent. At the same time, kids this age are increasingly aware of how others, especially their peers, see them and they're desperately trying to fit in.[7]

This scenario of secular adolescence as defined by identity conflict and peer group pressure does not correspond to the social or cultural configurations of most pre-contact Native North American cultures. Neither does it characterize the coming of age experienced by many Native girls. In both historical and contemporary contexts, American Indian girls' psychological, physical, and sacred senses of self often depend upon a merging of their identities with a powerful female spirit being such as Changing Woman (Navajo) or the Corn Mother, Selu (Cherokee) — or in the case of Pocahontas, Winona (Blossom), the daughter of Full Bloom.

The Woman Who Fell from the Sky

Paula Gunn Allen, who is Laguna Pueblo/Metis, radically revisions the legacy of Pocahontas, this most famous American Indian girl, by interpreting her life within an Algonquian rather than a Euro-American framework. This indigenous perspective challenges not only Strachey's hypersexual portrayal of Pocahontas but also the hegemonic representation of her as John Smith's adoring young paramour. Allen argues that Pocahontas, whose birth name was Matoaka, or "swan

---

7. "A Parent's Guide to Surviving the Teen Years," *http://kidshealth.org/parent/growth/ growing/adolescence.html.*

feather," received training as a Beloved Woman throughout her pre-pubescent years.[8] For Algonquian cultures, the swan feather signified *powa* — a special ability to perceive the para- and supernormal,[9] and the Mattaponi/Pamunkey people most likely recognized her extraordinary ability from birth. This insight gives new meaning to the swan feather carried by Pocahontas in the 1616 portrait by Simon van de Passe — the only representation of her known to have been engraved from real life.

According to Allen's provocative biography, Pocahontas/Matoaka earned the right to carry this feather in the midwinter Nikomis (Sky Woman) ceremony of 1608. The Sky Woman in this instance was Full Bloom, the Woman Who Fell from Above. Full Bloom's descent became the catalyst for earth's creation. Pregnant when she fell, Sky Woman soon gave birth to a daughter, whom she named Winona (Blossom). Eventually, Winona also conceived, but died when one of the twin boys could not wait to be born and tore a hole in his mother's side. Sky Woman used the body of her daughter to create the material world called Earth. In the midwinter ceremony in 1608, the child Pocahontas became the woman Winona: "This meant that in sacred time her head would become the new moon and her body the new sun and stars. So the cycle has ever continued, and the way of the Sky World, the *manito aki* or Other World, is always renewed"[10] Allen believes that, like many other Native rituals, the Nikomis ceremony was linked to astronomical events and constellations — and in this instance, to the waterbirds or "Swimming Ducks" constellation.[11] In pre-contact Algonquian cultures, Beloved Women were always marked by the presence of swan feathers, which functioned as a symbol of their connection to the waterbirds constellation.[12]

---

8. See Paula Gunn Allen, *Pocahontas: Medicine Woman, Spy, Entrepreneur, Diplomat* (San Francisco: HarperSanFrancisco, 2003), 31.

9. Ibid., 66.

10. Ibid., 45–46.

11. Western astronomers call this constellation Scorpio.

12. Allen, *Pocahontas*, 46.

She further notes that an important tenet of the Mattaponi/Pamunkey people signaled that when Sky Woman, through the waterbirds constellation, aligns herself again with earth — as she does "on a regular basis, sometimes thousands of years apart" — the world stands on the brink of massive change and renewal.[13] It was at the moment of this profoundly important synergy that Pocahontas metamorphosed into Winona and in the process remade Captain John Smith into a relative of Powhatan.

In spite of the continued perpetuation of the Pocahontas myth by film studios such as Walt Disney and the mass media more generally, many scholars have questioned the depiction of romantic love as the motivation of Smith's young savior. Allen situates Pocahontas's act specifically in the context of a Nikomis world renewal ceremony and her spiritual vocation as a Beloved Woman in training. One prerogative of Beloved Women was deciding the fate of captives. Smith, then the president of the Jamestown Company, had been captured while on a mission to locate the headwaters of the Chickahominy River. After six weeks of traveling to various villages, Smith's captors finally took him to Werowocomoco, the center of Powhatan's alliance and the site of the Nikomis ceremony that would decide the Englishman's fate. According to his own account (relayed in the third person):

> Before a fire upon a seat like a bedsted, he [Powhatan] sat covered with a great robe, made of Rarowcun skinnes, and all the tayles hanging by. On either hand did sit a young wench of 16 or 18 yeares, and along on each side the house, two rowes of men, and behind them as many women, with all their heads and shoulders painted red; *many of their heads bedecked with the white downe of Birds.* . . . A long consultation was held, but the conclusion was, two great stones were brought before Powhatan: then as many

---

13. Ibid., 46. In many communities, this ceremony has been and still is celebrated every year, but the years of the alignment between the waterbirds constellation and Earth take on a special significance.

as could layd hands on him, dragged him to them, and thereon laid his head, and being ready with their clubs, to beate out his braines, Pocahontas the Kings dearest daughter, when no intreaty could prevaile, got his head in her armes and laid her owne upon his to save him from death; whereat the Emperour was contented he should live to make him hatchets.[14]

We now know that Pocahontas was only eleven or twelve rather than the sixteen or eighteen conjectured by Smith. Even at this tender age, however, her father recognized her considerable authority as a Beloved Woman. Many historians now believe that Smith underwent a ritual signifying the death of the old self and his rebirth as a member of Powhatan's alliance.[15] Through her claiming of the captive, Pocahontas had, in effect, symbolically remade John Smith into a relative who possessed reciprocal responsibilities toward his new kin ("he should live to make him hatchets") — responsibilities that he unfortunately failed to fulfill. Rather than manifesting an adolescent crush on the handsome Englishman, then, her act worked to protect her people and ensure their survival.

Readers might now be thinking, "This is very interesting but how does it relate to our understanding of contemporary Native girls?" One of the most important lessons of Pocahontas is that for American Indian cultures, girls' sacred selves are situated in very different contexts than the modern psychological theory of adolescence would acknowledge. Indeed, many Native cultures still perform their own version of the Nikomis ceremony: the Kinaalda of the Navajo, for example, or the Isánáklésh Gotal of the White Mountain Apache. Besides this, the historical repression of Pocahontas's sacred self mirrors what too often is done to female American Indian "adolescents" both by non-Natives and even by their own communities.

14. Smith, in Karen Ordahl Kupperman, ed., *Captain John Smith: A Select Edition of His Writings*, Institute of Early American History and Writing (Chapel Hill: University of North Carolina Press, 1988), 64; emphasis added.
15. Ibid., 65, n. 20.

Unchanging Changing Woman

When Changing Woman gets to be a certain old age, she goes walking toward the east.[16] After a while she sees herself in the distance looking like a young girl walking toward her. They both walk until they come together and after that there is only one. She is like a young girl again.[17]

Many American Indian girls have experienced dislocation and alienation from their families and tribal heritages. The federally mandated project of detribalization through the dispersal of ancestral lands, the boarding school system, and the religious crimes code have all bequeathed high rates of poverty, unemployment, alcoholism, drug abuse, and domestic violence to almost every Native nation. In spite of this systemic assault on Native identity, however, some communities have asserted young women's sacred selves by continuing to celebrate coming-of-age ceremonies such as the Kinaalda. According to Apache scholar Inés Talamantez, the Kinaalda instructs Navajo girls to live their lives modeled after Changing Woman — who, like Sky Woman, created the human world. One of the most important and poetic parts of this four-day ritual is the "molding" ceremony. While a girl lies on a blanket in front of her hogan, or family dwelling, an older woman kneads her body and straightens her hair to make her shapely and beautiful.[18] This beauty is spiritual as well as physical: literally and symbolically "molded" into the sacred self of Changing Woman, Navajo girls become empowered through their participation in the Kinaalda.

The Apache have a similar ceremonial, the Isánáklésh Gotal or Changing Woman/White Painted Woman Sing, which is said to calm

---

16. For the Navajo as well as all other American Indian cultures, east is the direction of new life.

17. Keith Basso, quoted in Carolyn Niethammer, *Daughters of the Earth: The Lives and Legends of American Indian Women* (New York: Simon & Schuster, 1977), 47.

18. Niethammer, *Daughters of the Earth*, 46.

girls' adolescent imbalances: "The Mescalero conceive of 'fixing' the young initiate, ridding her of her baby ways and helping her through the door of adolescence, for at this young age the girls are said to be soft and moldable, capable of being conditioned and influenced by their female kin and others around them. Timid girls may need to be awakened to their female identities; others may need to be taught to settle down and be more sensible and feminine."[19] My point here is not to offer an ethnographic description of either the Kinaalda or the Isánáklésh Gotal. It is instead to present readers with one of the most important American Indian traditions for dealing with the throes of what is now called "adolescence": female coming-of-age ceremonies. In other words, Native North American cultures imbue young girls with sacred selves by facilitating their experiential identification with powerful spirit women: Sky Woman, Changing Woman, White Painted Woman, Selu, White Buffalo Calf Woman, and so on. As Talamantez notes, an Apache girl is not only temporarily transformed during the Isánáklésh Gotal; she is also permanently transformed into a mature embodiment of Changing Woman by the end of the ritual.[20]

Freud Meets Changing Woman

The Nikomis, Kinaalda, and Isánáklésh Gotal suggest that American Indian cultures have much to teach those non-Native psychologists and sociologists who have consistently underestimated the importance of ritual in human development. Perhaps what adolescent girls need is not more therapy but more ceremony. Perhaps Dr. Freud needs a good ceremonial sing with White Painted Woman rather than another session on the couch. One wonders how girls' lives might be changed if treatment professionals recognized that:

---

19. Inés Maria Talamantez, "The Presence of Isánáklésh and Apache Female Initiation," in *In Our Own Voices: Four Centuries of American Women's Religious Writing*, ed. R. S. Keller and R. R. Ruether (San Francisco: HarperSanFrancisco, 1995), 410.

20. Ibid.

I come to White Painted Woman,
By means of long life I come to her.
I come to her by means of her blessing,
I come to her by means of her good fortune,
I come to her by means of all her different fruits;
By means of the long life she bestows, I come to her;
By means of this holy truth she goes about.

—Morris Opler, cited in Niethammer, *Daughters of the Earth,* 48

Chapter 4

Latina Adolescents

Sliding between Borders
and the Yearning to Belong

DAISY MACHADO

I carry	*mis raíces*
my roots	*las cargo*
with me	*siempre*
all the time	*conmigo*
rolled up	*enrolladas*
I use them	*me sirven*
as my pillow	*de almohada*

—Francisco Alarcón

To tell the story of Latinas/os living in the United States — children, adolescents, or adults — one must talk about borders, one must talk about belonging and not belonging, one must talk about a history that has cast the Spanish-speaking population as outsiders, eternal foreigners whose place of birth does not matter because they will never truly belong. Pat Mora, Mexican American poet, whose birth in El Paso, Texas, identifies her as "Texican," describes this reality of life for Latinas/os in the United States as

the discomfort of "sliding back and forth between the fringes of both worlds." There probably isn't a week of my life that I don't have at least one experience when I feel that discomfort, the slight frown from someone that wordlessly asks, What is someone

87

like her doing here? But I am in the middle of my life, and well know not only the pain but also the advantages of observing both sides, ... of moving through two, and in fact, multiple spaces, and selecting from both what I want to make part of myself, of consciously shaping my space.[1]

Like Mora, I too know firsthand what it is like to move between these "multiple spaces." I came to the United States from Cuba when I was three years old. I did not grow up in the Miami of the 1960s but in New York City in the midst of a majority Puerto Rican population. So I was an outsider twice — not Puerto Rican and not Cuban because I had no Cuban community to help mirror the identity my parents shaped for me. Throughout my adolescence the question of my identity was a constant source of painful self-reflection. The Puerto Ricans reminded me I wasn't *puertorriqueña*; the whites reminded me that to them it did not matter what I was because my foreignness made me other, yet Cuba existed only in the stories my father told. I spoke English and despite my dominance of the language I always worried I had a Spanish accent. I also spoke both Spanish (filled with the vernacular of the Puerto Rican community that surrounded me) *and* Spanglish. And it was not until I was in my early twenties that, like Pat Mora and millions of other Latina/o youth, I began to acknowledge and embrace the contradictions of who I was and began to shape an identity that made me feel whole. In this process I finally claimed and celebrated my ability to be a linguistic and cultural border crosser.

The continuous sliding between borders, whether the borders are linguistic, cultural, racial, economic, social, or religious, is the daily reality of life for U.S. Latinas/os and it is in this place as outsiders and interlopers that Latino youth struggle to learn the skills they need to survive. Because they are truly not their mothers and fathers but are a new creation, they also struggle to give voice to their reality that is a hybrid identity they are creating.

---

1. Pat Mora, *Nepantla, Essays from the Land in the Middle* (Albuquerque: University of New Mexico Press, 1993), 6.

Hispanic youths were the fastest growing youth population in the 1990s, increasing by 56 percent among sixteen-to-nineteen-year-olds. In turn, Latinos represented a growing share of that population, increasing from 11 percent of the total sixteen-to-nineteen-year-old population in 1990 to 16 percent in 2000.[2] By 2020, it is projected that more than one in five children, from birth to eighteen years of age, in the United States will be of Hispanic origin.[3] Given this rapid growth, Latino youth are drawing increasing attention from government agencies, educational institutions, and foundations like the Pew Charitable Trusts, who are conducting research among Latino youth across the United States.

This chapter is an attempt to talk about Latina adolescents and to give voice to their reality and experience. The methodology used to begin this discovery is a conversation/interview I had with four Latina adolescents between the ages of fifteen and eighteen. I was able to gather this small group with the help of one of the adolescents whose mother is a friend of mine. I asked her if she could introduce me to a few of her friends who might be willing to sit and talk with me about what it means to them to be Latina in the United States. She asked around and we got together one afternoon and talked for about two hours. Before they came to the interview, I had asked each girl to answer some questions so I could have some concrete information to work with. I also asked them to adopt pseudonyms, and these are the names I will use to refer to them in this essay: Mariana, Valentina, Jewels, and Pebbles. In our time together we talked about them: What did it mean to them to be Latina? How did they see themselves fitting into the non-Latino society they lived in? What was it about being a Latina that made them proud but also brought them shame? What was the role and importance of religion in their lives?

---

2. Richard Fry, *Hispanic Youth Dropping Out of U.S. Schools: Measuring the Challenge* (Pew Hispanic Center, University of Southern California Annenberg School for Communication, June 8, 2003), 9.

3. *America's Children: Key National Indicators of Well-Being,* Federal Interagency Forum on Child and Family Statistics, 1998, 19.

It was a lively and honest conversation, and much to my surprise in this small group of four youngsters I found an accurate reflection of one of the most distinctive realities of the Latino community: into our communities enters a daily stream of immigrants from south of the border. Of the four adolescents I spoke with, two were Mexican Americans born in Texas and two were recently arrived immigrants from Colombia; together they represented the grating realities of the native-born and the foreign-born. These tensions were evident in the fact that the interview was conducted in English, Spanish, and Spanglish, that the issue of identity was a core subject, and that, even in this small group of youngsters, the struggle to belong was clearly visible even though it meant very different things to the Mexican American girls and to the Colombian girls. I will share their stories and insights and in doing so will afford the reader a glimpse of the reality faced by Latinas/os living in the United States. This conversation does not intend to be representative of the reality of all Latina adolescents, but it does represent some of the concerns and shared experience that most Latina adolescents face at one time or another. Because Latina/o reality, like any human reality, is so complex, I will focus on only a few main issues we talked about: identity, immigration, and religion. Of course none of these core issues stands alone; instead each weaves into the context of the others thereby creating the rich multilayered and complex texture of Latina/o life.

Identity

Jae-P is an L.A. rapper. He raps in Spanish and English, and like other rappers he tells the stories of life in his community, in this case life in a Latino inner-city barrio. The cover of his debut CD features a young Latino (Jae-P), head shaven, who stands between two cities. One is easily identified as Los Angeles with its tall downtown buildings. The other has a large Mexican flag and is the densely populated city of Tijuana, Mexico. Above Jae-P's head it says, *Dos mundos, dos lenguas, una voz* (two worlds, two languages, one voice). The hit single from which the CD is named is called "Ni de aquí, ni de allá" (not from here, not from there). While some African American rappers talk about gangsta life or police brutality, Jae-P expands the focus of his rap to include the ambiguity of Latino identity, the struggle of Latinas/os to explain who they are, the effort to learn English, the daily reality of low-paying service jobs, and the desire to belong in the face of the rejection by both the United States and Mexico. Jae-P has entered pop culture through rap music and has made his rhythm and rhymes a means to share the core predicament of Latinas/os — like Mariana, Valentina, Jewels, and Pebbles — living in the United States, the issue of identity. The chorus and first stanza of the rap "Ni de aquí, ni de allá" says the following:

> Porque no soy de aquí, ni soy de allá
> Pero aquí es adonde me gusta y me voy a quedar.
> Con dos acentos en la lengua llegaré a triunfar
> Te guste o no te guste a mí me van a aceptar...
> Ni mi cara ni mi piel fue la forma aceptada
> Made in USA, no valgo nada...
> Aunque hablo el idioma no crea que la hice
> Para el gringo soy un wetback, un simple chiste....
> Me vale lo que dicen, lo que dicen de mi...
> El latino de hoy en día no es un simple lavaplatos
> Hey Loreta Sánchez, ¿quién limpia tus zapatos?...[4]

> [I am not from here and not from there
> But here is where I like it and where I will stay
> With two accents on my tongue I will triumph
> Whether you like it or not you're going to have to accept me...
> Neither my face nor my skin is of the accepted type
> I was made in the U.S.A. but am worth nothing...
> Even though I speak the language don't think that I've made it

---

4. From the CD *Ni de aquí, ni de allá*, written by Byron Brizuela and Cecilia Brizuela, performed by Jae-P, Univision Records, 2003. The translation is mine.

To the gringo [Euro-American] I am a wetback, a simple joke...
But I don't give a damn what they say, what they say about me
Today's Latino is not just a simple dishwasher
Hey Loretta Sánchez, who shines your shoes?]

This small section of Jae-P's rap talks about some very important and emotional issues faced by Latina/o youth: not being the "right color" and not speaking the "right language"; the sense of rejection by Euro-Americans; learning to speak English (in this case with no accent) yet still not "making it"; having to deal with always being identified as an immigrant (legal outsider) even if, in Jae-P's case, he was born in the United States; being connected to the lower-paying service jobs such as dishwasher even though plenty of Latinas/os have achieved professional and managerial positions. He also makes a comment about Loretta Sánchez, a four-term congresswoman representing conservative Orange County (District 47) in southern California, an observation, perhaps, on the achievement of some native-born Latinos who obtain a certain economic and social status and then forget their identity and central concerns as Latinos. These are all issues that in some way or another touch the lives of Latino youth. Indeed, it is clear from Jae-P's lyrics that these same realities do not go unnoticed by Latino youth.

In my conversation with the four Latinas the issue of identity was very prevalent. When I asked the girls to tell me what it meant for them to be called Latina or Hispanic, this is what they said:

Jewels: The thing that comes to mind when I think about being Hispanic is that we work hard to survive. But being born here is still like, people still [say to me], "You were born in Mexico" no matter what. You're a wetback. I was born here and I know why I am here: I'm an American.

Pebbles: My mom taught me you're Mexican American. You know, born from this side, but sometimes they [Euro-Americans] think: born in Mexico. I'm like, "No, I'm born here." I've never been to Mexico. Well, I've lived here [Texas] all my life. I don't even speak Spanish with everybody, only my grandmother.

Mariana: Yo aprendí quién soy porque vengo de una cultura que ya, ya vengo con forma. ¿Sí me entiendes? Yo vengo de Colombia y allá crecí. Tenemos cultura y tenemos costumbres totalmente diferente [a las de aquí].

[I learned about who I am because I came already shaped by a culture. Do you understand? I am from Colombia, where I was raised. We have a culture and customs that are very different from what is here.][5]

As you can see from this short interchange, the two girls born in the United States and the other who migrated from Colombia understood identity in different ways. Identity for the two native-born Latinas is about ambiguity and the need for self-affirmation. They were sensitive to the fact that they had to explain themselves to non-Latinos, particularly to Euro-Americans, and they were vocal in affirming the fact that they were Americans. They were also aware that they were often assumed to be non-American or Mexican, which to many others means foreigner. The power of being labeled a Mexican must be noted because the label of foreigner places them in a category of otherness that they cannot understand precisely because they are not born in Mexico. Jewels's blunt statement, "I was born here and I know why I am here: I'm an American," is her self-affirmation, a reiteration that indeed she is where she belongs despite what white America may say. Perhaps what Jewels is not able to articulate because she herself has not become fully cognizant of it is the fact that both she and Pebbles represent a new definition of "American." Ed Morales, author of *Living in Spanglish: The Search for Latino Identity in America*, says this about the otherness imposed on U.S. Latinos:

---

5. Translations for all of the interview material are mine.

The problem for Latinos is that we are neither viewed as Americans — being consigned to a South of the Border ethos and all the foreign-tongued otherness that it implies — nor are we viewed as white, black or even Asian in the American race hierarchy. Even now, as bipartisan politics recognize that the country must confront its racial divide, Latinos are made invisible through negation. *Neither black nor white,* says the discourse on race — a perspective some Latinos take as a positive assertion that they lack the historical baggage of either group.[6]

Max Aguilera-Hellweg, a photojournalist who grew up on the U.S.-Mexico border, describes his reality as a Latino this way:

Growing up Mexican in America is to grow up an immigrant in one's own land. To be amputated at the hip without the language, without the culture, without a sense of history, continuity, or belonging to the rest of Latin America.[7]

While for the U.S.-born Latino being perceived as an "immigrant in one's own land" is a shared reality, for Latinas/os like Mariana and Valentina, who arrive in the United States from Latin America when they are in their late teens or as young adults, the issue of identity is about something different. For these Latin American immigrants who come with a sense of identity that has been shaped by their nation of origin, to live in the United States means a radical shift, because once they come to this country the identity imposed upon them is that of Latina/o or Hispanic. This imposed identity has nothing to do with being an immigrant because that is a category they understand and even embrace; after all they did migrate from their national homes and identify themselves as *colombianos, mejicanos, salvadoreños, venezolanos,* etc. They are immigrants from a specific nation with a specific

---

6. Ed Morales, *Living in Spanglish: The Search of Latino Identity in America* (New York: St. Martin's Press, 2002), 24, 25.

7. Max Aguilera-Hellweg, "La Frontera sin sonrisa," in *The Late Great Mexican Border: Reports from a Disappearing Line,* ed. Bobby Byrd and Susannah Byrd (El Paso: Cinco Puntos Press, 1998), 39.

culture. But arriving in the United States to discover that they have "become" a Latina/o or Hispanic is something totally unexpected and often unsettling; after all there is no other place in the world in which a Hispanic exists but in the United States. This imposed identity is one that is more often than not rejected by Spanish-speaking immigrants who, like most newly arrived immigrants, prefer to cling to their national identity and cultural roots where they find their true source of identity and sense of belonging.

That is why throughout the interview Mariana referred to herself as *colombiana* or Latina but not Hispanic. She claimed her national identity and could accept the name Latina because she understood it connected her to Latin America and the Spanish language, but she did not like or use the term "Hispanic." When asked whether she preferred to call herself Latina or Hispanic she responded,

> Yo me identifico como latina porque los latinos somos de Sur América. Soy colombiana y orgullosa.... Cuando llegué acá ya estaba formada...y el hecho que todo sea diferente aquí no significa que uno tenga o debe de cambiar...

> [I identify myself as Latina because Latinos are from South America. I am Colombian and proud.... When I arrived here I was already formed...and the reality that everything is different here (in the U.S.) does not mean that one has to or should change...]

Notice how Mariana takes the label "Latina" and redefines it so that it no longer holds the meanings implied by the larger U.S. culture. For her a Latina is someone from South America, someone with a distinct national identity, who speaks Spanish as her first language, and who now happens to live in the United States. Being Latina does not mean that she is no longer Colombian, and this redefinition and use of the term "Latina" is important to note. Being Latina for Mariana is a naming she has accepted on her own terms; in many ways it is an artificial identity that cannot supersede her true identity as a Colombian. For Pebbles and Jewels, being Latina is a more fluid label and implies a more ambiguous identity because they have no ties to any other nation to anchor them. So they call themselves Mexican American or simply American as ways to claim an identity. Yet at its very core this identity is in constant flux because to be Latina (or Hispanic) in the United States is to live a life that has been shaped by a distinct national historical imagination. Arturo Madrid, writing about identity and the Latino community, says that we are still in a particular place in the national consciousness:

> The U.S. communities labeled Latino are a diverse set of populations whose roots grow deep in the soil of the United States. Their members, however, have not either as individuals or as a collectivity, ever been considered part of the "imagined community" of this nation. We have been consistently defined out. . . . That is the subtext of the question all Latinos are asked: And where are you from? We are not perceived as being "from here." Rather, we have been considered to be a "foreign other," regardless of our individual or collective histories. Moreover, our imagined "otherness" is shaped by deep-rooted images and stories concerning our ancestors and ancestry. . . . We have been imagined and we have been found wanting.[8]

And this is the heartbreaking part of the story: the longer she lives in the United States the more Mariana will learn what her native-born Latina friends have already discovered: being Latina is to live in a third space and to experience an identity that "is involved in constantly struggling to emerge from the bottom-up."[9]

---

8. Arturo Madrid, "Alien, Misfits, and Interlopers: The Racialized Imagining of the U.S. Latino Communities at the End of the 20th Century," in *Race in 21st Century America*, ed. Curtis Stokes, Theresa Meléndez, and Genice Rhodes-Reed (East Lansing: Michigan State University Press, 2001), 100.

9. Antonia Darder, "The Politics of Biculturalism: Culture and Difference in the Formation of *Warriors for Gringostroika and the New Mestizas*," in *The Latino Studies Reader, Culture, Economy, and Society*, ed. Antonia Darder and Rodolfo D. Torres (Malden, Mass.: Blackwell, 1998), 138.

Immigration

The reality of immigration looms over all U.S. Latino communities and the immigration of youth is even more prominent. Large-scale immigration is one of the most important social developments of our time. It is a transformational process affecting families and their children. Once immigrants are settled, they send for their loved ones or form new families. Hence, the story of today's immigration is also a saga of children: a fascinating and critical — but too often forgotten — chapter of the immigrant experience.[10]

Statistics tell us that "thirty-five percent of Latino youth are immigrants, in comparison to less than five percent of non-Latino youth."[11] This demographic is one that cannot be easily dismissed because it points to a series of challenges to which U.S. institutions will have to respond.

Among the primary institutions in which one immediately feels the impact of such a large Latino youth immigrant population are the schools. Statistics show that Latino youth have a higher dropout rate (15 percent) than African Americans (12 percent) and white youth (8 percent). However, what is different about the dropout rate for Latino youth is the immigration factor. The Pew Hispanic Center at the University of Southern California conducted a national survey entitled *Hispanic Youth Dropping Out of U.S. Schools: Measuring the Challenge*, in which it was found that

in addressing the needs of young high school dropouts, educators need to be aware that the dropout populations have diverse demographic and labor force characteristics. Latino dropouts differ from white and African American dropouts in important ways.... Within the Latino dropout category, however, there

---

10. Carola Suárez-Orozco and Marcelo M. Suárez-Orozco, *Children of Immigration* (Cambridge: Harvard University Press, 2001), 1.
11. Fry, *Hispanic Youth*, 10.

are three populations that also have distinct variations: the U.S.-born and educated, the foreign-born who receive at least some education in the U.S., and the foreign-born who attend school in their home countries and emigrate primarily for work opportunities.[12]

Directly related to the success in education is the issue of language. The Pew study found that

English language ability is an important indicator for the likelihood of dropping out of high school among Latinos. Unlike most white and African American dropouts, Latino dropouts overall are not proficient English speakers.

Almost 40 percent of Latino high school dropouts, including recent immigrants who never attended U.S. schools, do not speak English at least "well." But English proficiency is fairly widespread among Hispanic youth. In 2000, about 86 percent of Hispanic sixteen-to-nineteen-year-olds either spoke only English or spoke English at least well. The 14 percent of Hispanic sixteen-to-nineteen-year-olds who have poor English language skills have a very high dropout rate. About 60 percent of these youth are high school dropouts.[13]

The issue of language remains a very important one for Latino youth. For the recent immigrant it is about the challenge to learn and master a new language in order to move ahead in life; for the native born it is about not losing Spanish or in some cases recovering the use of the Spanish language. A continuous undercurrent to the issue of language is that of belonging, and this idea of belonging happens on at least two levels. The first is the need to speak English in order to fit in to the school environment and to succeed in the United States. The second is the sense of ambiguity about Spanish

12. Ibid., 13.
13. Ibid.

because to keep it means to be further identified by whites as a foreigner (non-American) but to lose it totally means to be seen as not Latino by the immigrant community and by those who live in nations to which native-born Latino youth have some familial connections. This was the case for the two native-born adolescents I interviewed, as demonstrated in this exchange:

Pebbles: Well, with me, in school, even though I don't speak a lot of Spanish I have an accent. And people...make fun of my accent and it's like, I care less how you talk 'cause you have an accent too. Everybody has an accent, no matter what. You can have a Texan accent. You can have a country accent.

Jewels: And its not gonna make a difference. We all speak the same language, so we're all going to understand each another. Just knowing I can stick up for myself, knowing that even though you could make fun of me all you want, I'm still gonna speak the same language as you.

Pebbles: The thing that bugs me is that I don't speak Spanish well [enough]. When I try to help other people who need help [because] they talk Spanish I kind of feel I can't do that because I'm not that good of a Spanish speaker.

Jewels: To me it doesn't make a difference, but sometimes it does ...because people say to me, "Well, how are you going to be Hispanic and not know how to speak Spanish?" I'm trying my hardest to speak it.

Notice how the girls struggle to speak a "no accent" English so they can fit into the broader social settings they engage with, yet they also feel rejection from Spanish-speaking Latinos who criticize them because they do not speak Spanish. Also notice the ambiguity about not speaking Spanish. They are caught between two worlds — one that makes fun of them for speaking English with an accent and one that rejects them for speaking English (with or without an accent) and not speaking Spanish. The ambiguity of language is also reflected in the rap by Jae-P when he says, "Even though I speak the language don't think that I've made it." For Latino youth the solution to this complex issue of language has been found in the use of Spanglish.

Spanglish was something birthed out of necessity. There is a need for Latinos to assimilate in the United States, but we have always searched for a way to do that without losing who we are.[14] But for some Latinos Spanglish is even more than a hybrid language; it is a resistance to the push of assimilationists who question why Latinas/os will not "melt" in the great monocultural pot. Ed Morales, a journalist and activist, explains Spanglish this way:

> Generations of living in el Norte have allowed Latinos the space to begin to create a hybrid American culture that reflects the flexibility and absorptive ability of Latin America's.... Spanglish culture is not about segregation; its borders are permeable, but it has a strong core. If there is stability in the state of flux, it exists in a core that celebrates difference — permanently evolving, rapidly expanding difference.... The Spanglish idea rejects the halfhearted attempts by a litany of "multicultural conservatives" to promote assimilation as a way to enhance progress. Multicultural conservatives are multicultural only in name and not in practice — their goal is to reinforce the monocultural majority. *Living in Spanglish* does not promote assimilation, but rather suggests that North America begin its long overdue process of assimilation into the greater American hemisphere.[15]

Religion

Looking at religious affiliations in the United States we find that 47.7 percent of African American youth are Baptist; 55.7 percent of

---

14. Morales, *Living in Spanglish*, 26.
15. Ibid., 26, 29.

Hispanic youth are Catholic; 35.5 percent of Asian youth are Catholic, while another 11 percent are Buddhist. White adolescents are 22.7 percent Catholic, 20.3 percent Baptist, 7.1 percent Methodist, with the remainder distributed among many different traditions, each claiming less than 5 percent of the total.[16] The figures clearly show that Latino youth have the highest rate of self-identified religious affiliation (Roman Catholic), proving once again what U.S. Latina/o theologians have been consistently saying: Religion, with its important and life-affirming rituals and celebrations, remains at the core of the Latina/o community. What U.S. theologians are referring to is a particular expression of Roman Catholicism called "popular Catholicism." It is described by theologian Suárez Rivero like this:

> a major component of Latino cultural reality that has not been profoundly invaded by the Euro-American dominant culture. It still acts as indispensable bearer of values, traditions, symbols, and worldview for and within the U.S. Latino communities. The importance of popular Catholicism in the cultural self-definition and self-preservation of U.S. Latinos cannot be exaggerated.[17]

The importance of popular Catholicism in the life of the community is shown in the rituals and celebrations that bring people together around significant human events such as baptism (birth), *quinceañera* ("sweet-fifteen," marking entry into womanhood), weddings (family), *Día de los muertos* (Day of the Dead, celebration of life beyond death); *posadas* (Christmas celebration reminding the community of the poverty of the Christ child). There are also the feasts related to significant saints or the popular devotion to the Virgin Mary (such as the feast of Our Lady of Guadalupe for Mexicans and Mexican Americans or the feast of Our Lady of Charity for Cubans). These celebrations are

---

16. *National Study of Youth and Religion*, a four-year research project conducted at the University of North Carolina, Chapel Hill, funded by Lilly Endowment, Inc., begun 2000. See *www.youthandreligion.org*.

17. Ruy G. Suárez Rivero, "U.S. Latino/a Theology: A View from the Outside," in *From the Heart of Our People*, ed. Orlando O. Espín and Miguel H. Díaz (Maryknoll, N.Y.: Orbis Books, 1999), 244.

about daily relationships with one another and most importantly with the sacred, and it is in these celebrations that the stories (history) of the community is reaffirmed, identity is confirmed, and women be-come major protagonists because they are the main bearers of cultural identity and memory.

The four adolescents I interviewed were all Roman Catholic and all concurred that religion, their faith experience, was an important component of their lives. All agreed that religion was important to their families, and they each identified either their mother or grand-mother as being "very religious." They all attend Sunday Mass; one of the four said she also participated in the Wednesday night services, and another said she was active with her church's youth group. When asked to share their thoughts about the role of religion in their own lives, here is what two of the girls said:

Mariana: Hay muchas personas que para ellos la religión es muy importante, pero no la practican. Yo pienso que no vale la pena creer en algo y no practicarlo, la idea es creer y practicarlo; para así poder sentirse bien con uno mismo y con los demás. Aparte, si tienes fe y esperanza todo va saliendo a su debido tiempo.

[For many people religion is important, but they do not practice their religion. I think that it is not worth believing something and not practicing it; the idea is to believe and to practice that belief so one can feel good about oneself and good about others. Besides, if you have faith and hope things will work out in due course.]

Jewels: I think religion is very important, and in my family reli-gion has been a part of our lives for generations. My grandmother is very religious, but I have not reached that point of being com-pletely religious. I think you know when you are ready to give yourself to the Lord, you'll know.

Both adolescents agree that religion is important to them personally even though Mariana is more certain of the need to actively practice her faith and expresses a sense that her faith will improve her life's outcome. In comparing herself to her grandmother, Jewels finds that she is lacking in her religiosity but does admit to believing in a moment of conversion or a more personal encounter with God.

When asked what were the most significant religious symbols in their lives both Mexican American girls identified the Virgin of Guadalupe and the girls from Colombia identified the popular devotion found in their country to *El Divino Niño* (the Divine Child). The devotion to *El Divino Niño* leads us to another reality of religion in the U.S. Latina/o community: When people cross borders they bring with them their religious beliefs and practices. The devotion to *El Divino Niño* introduced by the Carmelites to Colombia in 1907 is an example of popular Catholicism. The first recorded miracle recognized by a bishop took place in 1915 and was the first of many. In 1937 Fr. Juan Rizzo, an Italian priest working in one of the poorest communities in Bogotá, began to think about how he could build a church building in such a poor community. After he asked for the help of the Divine Child his dream was realized in 1942 when a church building was erected and consecrated in this community as a physical reminder of the presence of God in the midst of the poor. The Divine Child, dressed in a simple pink robe, with a halo but no crown, stands on a cloud with his arms outstretched to the heavens and to all of humanity. The devotion uplifts the Christ child's innocence, simplicity, and unwavering love. For Mariana and Valentina the Divine Child is an important icon of their faith, their nationality, and their identity. They may be immigrants, but in *El Divino Niño* they maintain a connection not only to their national religious roots but also to the faith community they left behind. Valentina especially expressed how much she missed going to Mass in Colombia and missed not being able to celebrate with that community.

But religion is important to Latino adolescents not only as an aid in defining their identity and maintaining ties to family and culture. Religious practice has also been identified by social scientists as an aid to educational development and achievement. A study done by the Institute of Latino Studies at the University of Notre Dame called

Religion Matters: Predicting Schooling Success among Latino Youth asks the question: What role does religion play in protecting Latino youth from failing academically and in contributing to their educational success? The researchers conclude:

> As the United States moves toward a population that is one-quarter Latino, the educational successes and failures of the youngest Latino generation will play a pivotal role in what the Latino community and the United Sates become. The educational trajectory of the large number of young Latinos will shape their economic fortunes and social integration. . . . [In this study we have suggested] that religion plays an important role in the educational success of individual Latino kids. We have argued that church participation makes available resources embedded within social ties marked by trust and reciprocity (i.e., social capital) within congregations. Most of our findings are consistent with our claim that churches give Latinos social capital that contributes to educational success. We find that Latino students who actively attend church or who see their religious faith as very important to their lives are achieving higher grades in school, are staying on-track in school, are having less trouble with teachers, other students, and homework, and identify with school more strongly. Religious practice is especially important for the educational success of Latino youth living in impoverished neighborhoods.[18]

The religious practice of Latina/o youth should therefore not be dismissed or ignored. As the various research studies done by Notre Dame and the University of North Carolina show, religious belief and practice are indeed important components in the lives of Latino youth. In a world that more often than not dismisses religion and especially the

---

18. David Sikkink and Edwin I. Hernández, *Religion Matters: Predicting Schooling Success among Latino Youth* (Notre Dame, Ind.: Institute for Latino Studies, University of Notre Dame, January 2003), 41.

religious practices and beliefs of Latinas/os, labeling them as superstitious or backward, a word of caution is warranted. The U.S. Latino community continues to have and will have for generations to come at the very core of its being and identity a place for faith and practice, a place for the daily interruptions of the Divine.

Conclusion

The reality and shared experience of U.S. Latinos, whether native born or immigrants, is one filled with otherness, rejection, exclusion, and even invisibility. The many stresses, whether these are emotional, economic, or social, cause our Latino communities hurts and pains. Yet the Latino community has continued to forge ahead with this large and varied Latino youth population leading the way. As a member of the Latino community, I struggle with the labels imposed on me, with the foreignness ascribed to me, and with the neglect with which my people are treated. But I hold on to hope that is not only fed by my faith but also by the faith of my community. The four adolescents I interviewed represent me and are me and struggle like I do to make sense of it all, and I find hope and comfort in their youth and dreams. As the statistics presented in this article show, the Latino population in the United States is rapidly becoming a community that can no longer be ignored. This means that the black/white dichotomy, the preferred way to talk about race in this country, is even more of an artificial construct, and to continue to uphold it means to continue to negate the historical fact that Spanish-speaking mestizos have lived on what is today the United States mainland since the eighteenth century. This also means that we must engage in a new discourse that is borderless and permeable. I find hope-filled signs of this new discourse being produced by Latina/o youth, and it can be seen in the barrios where poverty and hope cohabitate, it can be heard in the rhymes and rhythms of raps in Spanish and English, it can be experienced in the art and murals, and it can be verbalized in the use of Spanglish. I think this is what Chicana poet and activist Gloria Anzaldúa was talking about when she wrote about *"mestiza* consciousness," because she envisioned Latinas as the ones who could carry forth this important task of bringing about change. I think Anzaldúa believed the women would lead the way because it is women who continue to remember, and in remembering they continue to birth a people with a history, a people with an identity, a people with hope. I conclude my chapter with this poem entitled "Remember," and I dedicate it to all the Latina adolescents across the many barrios of the United States, for they will continue to be the bearers of our future.

> Remember,
> who, how. Remember who you are.
> How did I get here?
> Remember your descendants.
> Remember your language.
> Remember who you are
> even when there's prejudice of who you are
> and what you are.
> Remember.[19]

---

19. Renato Rosaldo, "Surveying Law and Borders," in *The Latino Condition: A Critical Reader*, ed. Richard Delgado and Jean Stefancic (New York: New York University Press, 1998), 637.

Chapter 5

Love Letters in a Second-Hand Hope Chest

Working-Class White Girls Delaying Dreams and Expanding Soul

DORI GRINENKO BAKER

My Invisible Inheritance

Long before I ever heard the word "homeless," I knew a man named Bobby Fish. He was thin and wiry. He wore the same clothes day after day. I remember the earthy smell of the shed where he lived on my family's small farm, the way his fingers trembled, and the kind way his eyes would meet mine as he thanked me for the plate filled with steaming food.

At age ten, it was often my task to bring Bobby Fish his dinner. I would walk the short distance from our mobile home to the shed just before sitting down to eat my own dinner with my family. I never felt afraid of Bobby Fish. He was a man down on his luck. He was poor. I knew from the pile of aluminum cans we harvested for recycling that he drank a lot of beer.

Much later, I learned that Bobby had spent two years of his teenage life as a medic, pulling corpses from the battlefield in the South Pacific during World War II. Living with symptoms now called Post-Traumatic Stress Disorder, he never married and had no family. Bobby moved out of our shed when he became the live-in caretaker on a nearby citrus farm.

We lived in our yellow mobile home for only a year, while our new ranch-style brick home was being constructed. It gets awfully hot in a mobile home under the Florida sun, so we gladly unwound ourselves and our belongings from the cramped confines when our new house was ready. Bobby lived and worked at the nearby farm for years. When he became ill in his seventies, my dad helped him navigate the paperwork at the VA hospital.

When I was eleven, my aging grandfather moved in with us. The bus dropped me off an hour before anyone else got home. I never knew what to expect when I walked in the door. Sometimes Poppy would be sitting quietly on the couch. I would startle him from his reverie, and he would swoop his hand in a gracious wave to welcome me home. Other days he would be muttering in his native Russian, unable to recognize me. Once he stood with a puzzled expression on his face beside the open gate as the cows and sheep roamed freely about.

Eventually, Poppy's senile dementia required us to hire a sitter to ensure his safety when he was home alone. At the end, he spent a bed-ridden two years in a nursing home. Occasionally I would accompany my father — after he commuted home from his job as an inner-city social worker — on his daily pilgrimage to visit Poppy. We would drive twenty minutes to the nursing home, slowly bring spoonfuls of food to Poppy's lips, caress him, call him by name, and drive home. I remember sadly wondering how long life like this was supposed to last. I also remember the exhaustion on my father's face. My father was the son of two first-generation working-class immigrants. His father left Russia at age seventeen and sought work on rubber tree plants in Brazil and copper mines in the Upper Peninsula of Michigan before landing a job on the assembly line at the Ford Motor Company in Detroit. My grandmother emigrated to the United States at the age of two and completed her eighth-grade education before laying aside her aspirations to be a teacher so she could help with her nine siblings on a Minnesota farm. As a mother, she gave twenty-five cents a week to a door-to-door insurance salesman who confidently promised that the policy would mature into college tuition for her two sons. In fact, the policy ripened to a mere $500, but it had done its job. My dad knew he had no choice but to go to college.

I inherit three invisible but very present gifts from my father. I inherit from him a deep memory of radical hospitality, rooted in the immigrant experience of his parents and grounded by the liberal training he received as a social worker in the early 1960s.

I inherit a view of masculinity that differs from "manly man" images of the street fighters with whom he grew up and the testosterone-pumped mooks of my daughters' generation.[1] This masculinity includes taking care of the weak, extending the table of plenty, and abiding with one another through deeply troubling times.

I inherit an unearned privilege — a given birthright that comes with being born to parents of white, European ancestry.[2] While I was not articulate about matters of race, class, or gender as a white girl growing up in the South, I was aware that my life was less complicated than those of my Hispanic and African American classmates. Furthermore, having parents with college educations and professional lives added a layer of class privilege beyond that conferred by my skin color.

This cluster of privileges came with the knowledge that my life had claims upon it. Serving others was central to a life well-lived, and my accomplishments would be weighed in light of that value. Although our once-a-year visit to the Russian Orthodox Church failed to instill in me a connection to the Holy, witnessing my father's life of service

---

1. The "mook" is a term popularized by the PBS Frontline video "The Merchants of Cool." It refers to what critics call the "crude, loud, obnoxious, in-your-face character that can be found almost any hour of day or night somewhere on MTV. He's a teen frozen in permanent adolescence." Source: *www.pbs.org.* PBS Video "The Merchants of Cool," original airdate: February 27, 2001. Produced by Barak Goodman and Rachel Dretzin directed by Barak Goodman, written by Rachel Dretzin, correspondent and consulting producer Douglass Rushkoff. A Frontline Co-Production with 10/20 Productions, LLC.

2. Peggy McIntosh, "White Privilege: Unpacking the Invisible Knapsack," excerpted from *White Privilege and Male Privilege: A Personal Account of Coming to See Correspondences through Work in Women's Studies,* Wellesley College Center for Research on Women, Working Paper 189, 1988. Excerpts from this paper can be found at *www.whiteprivilege.com.* See also "White Privilege Shapes the U.S." by Robert Jensen, *Baltimore Sun,* July 19, 1998, which can also be read at *http://uts.cc.utexas.edu/~rjensen/freelance/whiteprivilege.htm.*

to others prepared me for the day when, at age fifteen, my soul heard an ancient story about a man who spent his life feeding the hungry and caring for the disenfranchised.

This inheritance, often unacknowledged, accompanied me on my journey into Christianity. My Christian walk began in naive acceptance, awakened to struggles over the church's long history of patriarchal oppression of my gender, and eventually led to an ongoing awareness of my white, middle-class, heterosexist upbringing as primary and limiting lenses through which I view the world.

Coming to understand and unmask these privileges is a process that feels very much like unwinding myself from the cramped confines of the trailer I lived in as a pre-teen. Living in tight spaces, you learn how to get by. You forget how to expand. Each new learning about gender, race, class, and heterosexism — always filtered through the storied universe of Christianity — leads me to a place with a little more room to stretch, a little more air to breathe, and a wider horizon for being in relation to others. These movements have led me to align myself with other faithful Christians who engage in the struggle of reconstructing church and theology in ways that confront much of its past.[3] This is often a painful task because it means letting go of ways that are comfortable, custom-made to fit, and often largely unquestioned because they are so invisible.

It is my history — as one white girl who grew up in the South, in a particular family with its own complexities — that I bring to the issues this book examines. When asked to look for traces of spirituality in the hard lives of working-class white girls, I brought with me my own experiences as a ten-year-old daughter, an eleven-year-old granddaughter, a fifteen-year-old girlfriend, and a grown woman who learned to define herself beyond those male-identified ways of being. I held the knowledge that each girl I met would be just as thickly formed by her race, her class, her gender, and a complex web of other relationships. Partly

---

3. Rebecca S. Chopp and Mark Lewis Taylor, *Reconstructing Christian Theology* (Minneapolis: Fortress, 1994), 8.

out of concern for my own daughters, who will come of age and forge their own spiritualities within the Bible-Belt South, I decided to listen to girls close to home, in Altavista, Virginia, the small town where I live.

As I listened to these girls, I found that spirituality is tangled up with sexuality, economics, and feelings of freedom and bondage. Their spirituality groans under the weight of dreams they have had to delay. It is deeply rooted in their experiences with men. It is thoroughly tinged with the fundamentalist Christianity of church and Bible-Belt culture. And it constantly longs for something more. I found that — like love letters stored in a second-hand hope chest — girls' understandings of God can sustain a lingering visit, a process of opening, sorting, keeping, and discarding that can be at the same time both painful and liberating.

Changing Hopes in the Town of Hope Chests

"This town is so small that a friend of mine, she kissed a boy at the Food Lion, and by the time she got to McDonald's, everybody knew about it," said Jo, fifteen.

Jo's anecdote was told with dramatic flair. But the nods of agreement and affirmations of "uh-huh" offered by the other girls around the table testified to its veracity. "That *really* happened," sixteen-year-old Amy chimed in, as if to underline the incredulity of a place where everybody's business is so mixed up with everyone else's. The town where we live is *that* small. Altavista, Virginia, quite literally begins with the town's only chain grocery store and ends a brief mile and a half down State Road 29 with a fast-food restaurant.

In between is the former headquarters of a furniture company that once exported its signature product — the moth-free, heirloom-quality Lane Cedar Hope Chest — to the homes of young women all over the world. In its heyday, Lane employed thirteen hundred hourly wood-workers here.[4] On the outskirts of town is a once-thriving textile mill

4. I am grateful to the Minnie and Bernard B. Lane Foundation of Altavista for a generous grant that allowed me to conduct this research. This family's philanthropy

that now employs only a skeleton crew. In huge fertile tracts of land surrounding the town stand tall wooden barns used to dry tobacco, remnants of the once-lucrative family farms.

In the past six years, jobs in manufacturing fled to Indonesia and Mexico due to changes in international trade laws and the dynamics of a global economy. Increased awareness of the dangers of smoking and class-action lawsuits aimed at cigarette manufacturers caused tobacco to lose its allure. As a result, the region's farmers lost the assurance that hard work would lead to sufficient income. These simultaneous economic losses set into force a ripple effect. Restaurants closed, construction slowed, and retail sales dipped, causing employment in these sectors to lag during 2004, the year I collected the stories that follow.

As the silver-haired mayor of the town told me, while we sat on the white steps of the First Baptist Church awaiting the town's annual fireworks show, "This used to be a working *man*'s town. You knew if you dropped out of high school, you could still find a job and be able to earn a decent living" (emphasis added).

Clearly, this is no longer the case. It is not a man's town: in the United States today, women are more likely than men to achieve the primary marker of the ability to earn a decent living — a college diploma.[5] And dropping out of high school affords only a service-sector future, less than full-time employment with few chances of benefits at an employer such as Wal-Mart, which will soon open on the outskirts of town.

I decided to listen to girls in *this* town because it is where I live, work, and seek to build community. I did not go seeking *representative* views. I simply wanted to understand the church and God as seen through the unique and highly particular lens of being young, white, working class,

---

has enabled a state-of-the-art interracial YMCA that functions as the heartbeat of this community. In addition, the family's diligence in securing ongoing economic investment in the region has been instrumental in providing jobs that have kept families intact and social support networks in place for many.

5. U.S. Department of Education, National Center for Education Statistics (2005). "Postsecondary Institutions in the United States," Fall 2003 and Degrees and Other Awards Conferred: 2002–03 (NCES 2005-154).

and female in this small blue-collar town amid the economic changes occurring during the first five years of the twenty-first century.

What does God look like when you are the first person in your extended family to attend college? What does it mean to become self-sufficient at eighteen, working at the local grocery story and putting dreams of higher education on hold? How is your faith tested when you go part-time to the community college, as your friends move away to prestigious universities? How does a girl bring her realities, hopes, and visions to birth in light of the invisible constructs of race, class, and gender that affect her?

Starting with one teenager I knew well, I recruited a group of girls who come from families with deep roots in this region. Their "social ecological nests" vary.[6] They are the daughters and granddaughters of people who worked the line at the furniture company. They are the people whose families hold tracts of tobacco land passed down through generations, people who teach school, drive school buses, deliver mail, work in construction, or are unemployed. The homes they come from range from modest brick ranches to small apartments. Some of the households are run by stable, working, single mothers buffered by a supportive network of extended family and friends. Some of the families are more akin to what Tex Sample calls "hard-living," those who, due to material conditions of poverty and lack of supportive networks, live on the edge that divides the haves from the have-nots.[7] Still others had recently experienced a change in socio-economic status due to a parent's unemployment.

I found young lives plagued by absent fathers, betraying boyfriends, backbiting girlfriends, needy stepmothers, chaotic households, unplanned pregnancy, and — the most painful to report — sexual abuse by a church professional. In the midst of these painful places, their personal

---

6. Pamela D. Couture, *Seeing Children, Seeing God: A Practical Theology of Children and Poverty* (Nashville: Abingdon, 2000), 24.
7. Tex Sample, *Hard Living People and Mainstream Christians* (Nashville: Abingdon, 1993), 12.

struggles intertwine with political forces accompanying a downward spiral in the U.S. manufacturing base.

As I came to know these girls and their stories, I assumed a certain theological stance: I saw myself as a companion in search of windows to freedom from the psychological, physical, emotional, and spiritual bondage of sexism, abuse, white privilege, and patriarchy. The first step in such a liberatory hope is often naming the wrongs of a current situation. Even this small step of critically reading one's context implies an emancipatory vision. In order to reach toward a better life, one must hold — however tender and inchoate — an out-there, hoped-for belief in the possibility of one's own flourishing.[8]

As the girls gathered each session, they happily chatted about events of their lives — the upcoming basketball tournament, a week-end school theater production, a dispute with an employer. But as they told the stories adults rarely ask to hear, they revealed lives laden heavily with loss. Out of their losses we teased threads of a reliable and liberatory hope that is native to the particularities of coming of age as a working-class white girl in this blue-collar town.

The Research Method

Each time we gathered, a girl brought a story from her life that she had written and shared with me in advance. The group then took part in a four-step method I call Girlfriend Theology, designed to foster theological reflection on lived experience.[9] The method is an adaptation of action-reflection models of religious education that grow out of liberation theologies. I use it as both a research method and an intervention. As a research method, it aims at uncovering indigenous spiritualities. As an intervention, I am a caring, adult presence ready to give support and offer occasional alternatives to theological views

8. Evelyn Parker, *Trouble Don't Last Always: Emancipatory Hope among African American Adolescents* (Cleveland: Pilgrim Press, 2003), 151–53.

9. Dori Grinenko Baker, *Doing Girlfriend Theology: God-Talk with Young Women* (Cleveland: Pilgrim Press, 2005), 33–36.

that have been uncritically embedded and may not serve human flourishing.[10] I recruited an adult woman to participate with me in each of the eight sessions. I then transcribed the sessions and listened for themes that arose repeatedly.[11]

Emergent Themes and the Joy of Indigenous God-Talk

I heard the girls voicing two predominant, recurrent themes. Growing from — or sometimes in reaction to — these themes were a multitude of images of God, several of which I will share. The recurrent themes were:

+ rage over the seemingly endless cycle of broken relationships they have experienced with men, especially fathers and boyfriends. They hope for nonabusive, loving, intimate relationships with the opposite gender.

---

10. I use this method, rather than traditional interviews or focus groups, because I am intrigued by the stories girls *choose* to tell to others when given the invitation. More often than not, the stories are ones they *have not* told before. Unlike the rehearsed and scripted "testimonies" I heard on Wednesday nights as a guest in the Southern Baptist churches of my teenage friends, these stories are often fresh, unrehearsed, and raw. I look to this kind of story-sharing to revive and reshape the Christian practice of testimony. Rather than a private act of constructing one's story, testimony here becomes a communal act — the act of telling the truth of our lives out loud to one another. When seen this way, testimony becomes an especially important Christian practice for girls involved in the search for God in a dominant culture that often does not affirm their ways of knowing and being. For more on story sharing methods of religious education, see Ann Streaty Wimberly, *Soul Stories: African American Christian Education* (Nashville: Abingdon, 1994). For more on the Christian practice of testimony, see Dorothy Bass and Don C. Richter, *Way to Live: Christian Practices for Teens* (Nashville: Upper Room Books, 2002); Dorothy Bass, ed., *Practicing Our Faith: A Way of Life for a Searching People* (San Francisco: Jossey-Bass, 1997); and Thomas G. Long, *Testimony: Talking Ourselves into Being Christian* (San Francisco: Jossey-Bass, 2004).

11. Each session was taped and transcribed with the participants' permission. The girls and women were paid for their time, and each gathering closed with informal talk over pizza and soda. By the end of our six sessions together, we had become comfortable sharing details of our personal lives. The girls' names and any identifying characteristics have been changed to protect their anonymity.

♦ grief over the loss of their childhoods brought on by the struggle to make a living and the fragility of a family's equilibrium. They wish for a reprieve from grown-up responsibilities and a stable, comfortable homeplace in which to be lavished with parental supervision, nurture, and support.

As these themes surfaced through numerous stories, our discussions invariably ended with playful talk about how God might look and feel quite different from the God portrayed in church on Sunday morning or through the televised evangelism that seeps through the airwaves.

When these indigenous images of God surfaced, the joy was almost palpable. I concluded that — like thirsty wilderness survivors in a mostly barren land — these girls hope against hope for alternatives to the predominant image of an all-powerful and often punishing God they have soaked up from their surrounding Christian fundamentalist culture. They welcome new images of a God who loves unconditionally, embraces us in our particularity, and forgives deeply — over against a God who keeps a scorecard of mistakes and doles out punishment in the guise of random life events. These images of God come from the deep particularities of the girls' lives. For this reason, I call them indigenous and context-specific: They grow and expand naturally here when given the fresh air and sunshine of open, nonjudgmental theological reflection.[12]

The remainder of this chapter will focus on stories the girls told, the way these themes emerged from the stories, and the indigenous images of God that arose.

Rage over Broken Relationships with Men

Several stories brought to the surface expressions of rage over the seemingly endless cycle of broken relationships girls have experienced with men, especially boyfriends and fathers.

---

12. Patrick O'Connell Killen and John de Beer, *The Art of Theological Reflection* (New York: Crossroad, 1997).

The story "My Life in This Box," was told by Cat, a high school senior who identifies herself as a devout Christian. Cat had grown up as an active member of a self-described conservative, independent, "King James Version, Bible-believing," rural church. Cat was in the midst of a personal trauma throughout the weeks we met. A year earlier she had been the victim of persistent sexual abuse by one of the pastors of her church. After months of turmoil, she had reported the abuse, had received a court-appointed counselor, and was preparing to testify at the upcoming trial. Her family had since left the church. With that, Cat lost many lifelong relationships with people who she felt now doubted her allegations. Six months after our research was completed, the perpetrator pleaded guilty to the charges and was fired from his church job.[13]

After agreeing to be part of the group, Cat hinted that her story was "too painful to tell." When I sought her privately, she told me about the abuse and the pending court case. She asked about choosing a story to tell, saying, "There are so many stories I could tell. I have had to grow up too fast." I advised her to bring a story that was not directly related to the current crisis she was enduring.[14]

Reference to the abuse, its effect on her understandings of God, and the upcoming trial slipped into each session. Cat's having undergone such a serious violation at the hands of a church-worker she had trusted shadowed all of our conversations. As a researcher, I considered the impact her experience would have on the group. I weighed the ethical choices of keeping her in the group because it could be of

13. Despite decades of awareness education in Protestant churches about the dangers of clergy sexual abuse, girls and women often hesitate to report the abuse for fear of being blamed. See Marie Fortune, *Is Nothing Sacred?* (Cleveland: Pilgrim Press, 1999). Information about retreats, conferences, and seminars for women recovering from clergy abuse, as well as for professional education regarding clergy ethics and boundaries, can be found at *www.advocateweb.org*.

14. In practicing this method of storied theological reflection, I advise participants to avoid discussing a traumatic event that is still in process. Although acknowledging that traces of any ongoing trauma will show up in our conversation, I encourage stories that do not currently require therapy and am careful to refer participants to qualified professionals for crisis intervention.

value to her, versus removing her from the group because her voice might "skew" the findings. In the end, I decided her witness to the potential for evil within the church was important, as was the healing voice of her comrades, who offered tangible support in the face of an almost overwhelming crisis.[15]

When it was time for her story, Cat read as we listened.

My story starts about two years ago. Is that a long time? No, but it sure does feel like it. Two years ago is when my dad met his second wife, Sandy. At first, before they were married, things were okay between she and I. I mean...they weren't great, but they weren't bad either. As the wedding day approached though, something began to happen. I slowly began losing my dad, and she started treating me different. I have never looked at her like a mom. She came into my life too late for me to even begin to look at her like a mom. She is my "stepmom." That's what you'd call her, right? Well, when I introduce her as that, she would get angry and go to my dad upset about it. That made my dad angry because I had upset his wife. So he would come to me and lecture me on treating her better, which made me mad because I didn't feel like I had done anything wrong. I had simply called her my stepmom. I could have called her my "father's wife," but I figured that *would* be mean. It's one of those "damned if you do, damned if you don't" type of things, I guess.

Well, I closed myself off from them both for a while because I was sick of getting in trouble for what I felt was nothing. My dad came to me several times asking me to talk to him more...and I would give in. I would go to him with problems and issues that "daddy's girls" (which is what I was) go to their dads with. He just seemed never to be listening. After a while he really just stopped

15. For discussions of ethics in ethnographic research see Ruth Behar, *Translated Woman: Crossing the Border with Esperanza's Story* (Boston: Beacon Press, 1993) and *The Vulnerable Observer: Anthropology That Breaks Your Heart* (Boston: Beacon Press, 1996); Kamala Visweswaran, *Fictions of Feminist Ethnography* (Minneapolis: University of Minnesota Press, 1994).

having anything to do with me. I figured that he had five other kids to worry with. I am the oldest... so he can just let me go. I thought that for a while and then decided maybe I was being too rough on him. After all, he has been through a lot.

Until one night about a month ago. I had just gotten home from soccer practice. My dad was helping my little brother with his homework. I walked the steps to go to my bedroom and my dad, without taking his gaze from the homework said, "Hey, Baby." I replied, saying, "Hi, Dad."

I didn't realize that he wasn't talking *to me* until after I had replied. My father — the man who everyone knew thought of me as "his girl" — looked at me and said, "Oh, I thought you were Sandy" and turned his gaze back to the book. I felt about ten emotions all at one time. Several of which were anger, hurt, and sadness. I didn't say anything to him. I knew that if I did I would end up in trouble. So I just went to bed, realizing that what I had felt all along about losing my dad was true. I don't feel like "daddy's girl" anymore. Although my dad is still here on earth, I feel as though he were really gone. I think that of all the things that I have ever been through, the realization of no longer having a relationship with someone I love so dearly hurts more than anything else. I hope that one day I can become my daddy's girl again, but until then, I will just live one day at a time... hoping.

As Cat's voice tapered off, group members were quick to share their feelings of sadness for Cat as she experienced being replaced in her father's heart. They also shared disbelief around the expectations of the stepmother. They empathized with Cat and agreed that they would not have been able to call the stepmom "Mom." Cat shared that her biological mother had been a distant figure in her life, releasing custody to Cat's dad when she was a toddler.

After a while, the discussion turned back to her father. How could he be so insensitive and blind to his daughter's feelings? As the girls discussed the emotions the story triggered for them, they all agreed that Cat was grieving the loss of a relationship that had been central to her identity as "daddy's little girl." They empathized with what it must feel like to have to lose that particular part of her identity at the very time when she was preparing to graduate from high school. "I remember, at the end of elementary school, having a walk-through tour of the middle school. I need that now for what comes next. Only, my family isn't even aware of how scary this is," Cat said.

As the conversation deepened to revolve around relationships with men, the girls began to engage in an outpouring of emotions about fathers who had fallen short on their promises or boyfriends who proved untrustworthy. The girls chimed in with their own very personal stories of disappointment: "My father was never there for me," one girl said. "Mine neither," echoed another, tears streaming down her face.

Two girls who had positive memories of their fathers and boyfriends empathized with the girls expressing anger and rage. Even those who had experienced mostly positive relationships with men agreed that, despite their longing for stable, loving relationships with the males in their lives, they had "huge trust issues." When Cat said "I have built a thick wall of protection to guard my heart from being ripped out and stomped on," they all nodded their heads in agreement.

When the talk shifted to images that the story called to mind, I thought of the classic children's picture book *Are You My Mother?* by P. D. Barnes. I asked if anyone remembered the book about the little bird who falls out of her nest and embarks on a lengthy pursuit to find her mother. I described the climax of the book, a scene where the bird opens her mouth and screams at the top of her lungs, "I must have a mother. WHERE IS MY MOTHER?" At this point, the talk became very animated as several participants remembered the story and connected with the little bird's rage over not being able to find the nurture and support she knew she was due.

"It's like we all hope for a nest, a home, someone to nourish and feed us," Beth said. The talk kept drifting back to the image of Cat as a child, safe within the image of herself as "daddy's little girl." The hope in the story was that somehow she would find a place that felt like home.

As we moved into naming images of God that surfaced through the story, a profound awareness seemed to dawn on Cat. She realized that she rarely had the ability to talk about her feelings without censoring them for fear of becoming embroiled in an unwelcome family dispute. She looked back over the conversation of the last hour and named an "Aha" moment.

> *Cat:* Talking here felt different. Totally different. I have my granny. Granny listens to me with ears open wide. I couldn't ask for a better person: she's my rock. *But to have people I haven't known listen to me — now that was pretty cool, to not have to say, well I'm sorry for the way I feel.* (emphasis added)

> *May:* Don't ever say that to anybody! I think.

> *Cat:* I'm glad you all didn't say, well, you're wrong in feeling that way because that's what I've been told. I am living in this box.

Cat agreed that a good name for the story would be "My Life in This Box." The image of God that arose for her during this session was this: "The opportunity to talk about my life in a safe space feels different. God is like a safe space where I don't have to watch what I say and feel."

Although Cat's story was not directly about the events surrounding her experience of sexual abuse and the trial for which she was preparing, those events were deeply entangled in the complex web of issues she faced with her family. The hard work of reestablishing her identity in the wake of a crisis involving her body, a trusted mentor, and her faith community made it especially important to reconnect, if only briefly, with a God of safety.

Grief over Fast-Track Childhoods

Several of the stories turned to life events that caused nostalgic visions of childhood to flee swiftly. One story particularly released a flood of talk about being forced to grow up too fast. The girls in my research group grieved what they saw as an accelerated loss of their childhoods, and they hope for a reprieve from weighty, grown-up responsibilities.

The story "All Grown Up, Way Too Fast" was told by May, who comes from a family of hard-working manual laborers whose skill had been highly valued in the booming home-construction era of the late 1990s. Wealthy East Coast families building multimillion dollar vacation houses on a nearby lake resort had kept the family business in steady demand during the recent past. That ended when houses dotted each lot along the lakeshore. There was no place else to build. It was then that May's father became unemployed. When two infants were added to the household, May found herself in a chaotic environment. Typically witty and sarcastic, May cried as she read her story to us.

I don't think that my brother, only a senior in high school, was too thrilled to find out that his girlfriend was pregnant. She was only a sophomore (the same grade as me at the time). I'm sure they both experienced a range of emotions similar to those of the many other people that this upcoming event would inevitably affect. Luckily, they did the responsible thing, got married, moved in together (in our house first, then they got an apartment).

My brother had a good job and contributed all the money he could. His girlfriend got her GED, and unlike so many other teen parents, they have never been on welfare. However, somewhere in there they managed to do the not-so-responsible thing again and now there are two babies. The oldest is a beautiful baby girl who is now seventeen months old and the youngest, a baby boy who is five months today. Unfortunately, life sucks sometimes, and people like to make things hard. That's exactly what the in-laws did, and because of it my brother and his girlfriend had to move away to get a fresh start and to save their relationship.

In order to do this, they had to leave their kids behind with us in hopes that they could prepare a good home for them. It's been almost three months since they left. So, now all because

of some bad decisions and some jealous, sucky, meddling insti-
gators, my brother lives halfway across the country, I never see
him, and on top of that the stress level at my own house has
skyrocketed. Things are terribly busy, and it seems like there's
always a screaming match going on. I really admire my brother
for doing what he thinks is right, and my family for sticking this
out ... so far.

At the end of May's story, my adult collaborator rushed in immediately to share her feelings. She supported May for talking about what
was obviously still very painful.

Katie: I admire you and your parents for taking them in. You're
still in high school and you are forced to be so much for these
kids, while you should also still be kind of a kid yourself.

May: It's a five-kid house. We're trying to get me a car so I can
get to work, and trying to pay for the kids. It sucks, sucks, sucks.
Sometimes I just want the chance to enjoy my friends, a Friday
night out, without having to worry about adult responsibilities —
and these little kids are calling me Mom.

Although there has been a decrease in teen pregnancy, birth, and
abortion in the United States over the past decade, May's story was a
familiar one to these girls. At least one other girl in their four-hundred-
student high school had given birth the year before. According to
the Centers for Disease Control, when teens give birth, their future
prospects decline. Teen mothers are more likely to drop out of high
school, more likely to become single parents, and more likely to live
in poverty than other teens.[16]
The other girls in the group commiserated with May for having the
huge responsibility of helping to raise two children who were not her
own. At one point, Cat looked at May and said, "We both had to grow

---

16. "Trends from 1976–2003 in Pregnancy, Birth and Abortion Rates in Teens 15–17
Years," *Morbidity and Mortality Weekly Report*, February 4, 2005 / 54(04); 100.

up too fast." Turning to look at a mutual friend who recruited them both into the group, Cat said, "How come you didn't introduce her to me months ago? We're living the same life here!" They swapped impressions of living in chaotic households in which it seemed rare to have solitude or a peaceful, stress-free exchange with adults.

Katie shared that God's presence in the story was somehow wrapped up in the fact that, despite the family's hardships, they were struggling through the difficult time together. May mentioned that it was hard to imagine a positive outcome.

As we prepared to close our conversation and underline any moments of clarity, I mentioned the heaviness of the story and asked May how she was feeling. May said, "Somehow it feels lighter. It doesn't mean anyone is going to fix it, but it does feel lighter." I wondered aloud if that was an image for prayer. "Is prayer like the act of telling your heavy story to a listening friend? Can you envision a better outcome, even if it's very far away?" There were thoughtful expressions around the circle as the girls tried on the idea of talking to one another as a form of prayer. I glanced down and noticed that Beth had been holding May's hand throughout the entire session, a quiet act of solidarity throughout a tearful passage.

Indigenous Images of God

Distinct images of God, prayer, or spirituality surfaced from each story and our conversation around it. In Cat's story, God was like a "safe space where I don't have to watch what I think and feel." In May's story, prayer was considered as akin to the act of sharing a painful story with others who hear it and help imagine a positive outcome. In a third story, which was about a boyfriend who became verbally abusive, God was "like an armor one builds to protect her vulnerable self from being hurt."

Each of these images of God, prayer, or spirituality was embraced by some or all of the girls, who seemed to find the process of naming God as exhilarating as it was unfamiliar.

One last story provided occasion for the girls to practice the process of naming God with images from their natural surroundings. Jo told a story about a morning her boyfriend gave her an incredible gift. The group entitled it "The Day the Sun Rose Just for Me."

I'm a daydreamer. I love poetry, flowers, clouds, sunrises and sunsets....I am a lover of beauty. I am also definitely a sentimentalist. Luckily, I have the perfect boyfriend, who is a definite romantic. This summer, he and my family were camping at my family's small lake, which is right at the foot of Johnson Mountain....He had brought his four-wheeler and he, my sister, her friend, and I all took turns gallivanting about on it. All night he kept telling me that he had a surprise. I am by nature an extremely impatient and curious person, so needless to say, I begged and begged for him to tell me the surprise. Now, I must admit, I am quite spoiled, especially by him and usually, with enough begging, I get my way. However not this time! He refused to tell me the surprise. When we all retired for the night I was still wondering.

The next morning, I was awakened at five o'clock in the morning by someone singing "Good Morning, Beautiful" by Steve Holy in my right ear. I jerked awake and smiled at my boyfriend.

"Come on!" he whispered. He pulled me out of the camper and down the hill where he had the four-wheeler parked and running. On the back of the four-wheeler were a few blankets. I looked at him questioningly. He smiled, handed me my helmet, and beckoned for me to climb on. I did so and just minutes later we were roaring up the side of the mountain.

It was wonderful. I'm not sure much else wakes you up like flying up a mountain at five a.m. on the back of a four-wheeler with the wind whipping your hair and stinging your eyes. About fifteen minutes later, we were at the top of the mountain. My boyfriend helped me down and spread a few blankets on the moss-covered earth. We sat down and moments later, a huge, orange fireball appeared over the crest of the mountain. As it rose slowly I felt as if my whole body was being engulfed in a warm, tingly sensation. It felt as if the entire world was stopped, just frozen in that very moment where the sun was just rising and the birds were just waking up and gracing us humble humans with their song, singing the world a good morning song. There was a soft breeze blowing, just enough to stir my tousled hair and wrap me in the fragrance of crisp mountain mint. As I looked down from the mountain unto that sunrise, my whole world felt complete and perfect. I am sure that for the rest of my life, I will never forget that sunrise on Magic Mountain, as I affectionately dubbed it.

As we conversed around Jo's story, there was a lightness that had not been present during many of the sessions that had dealt with sadder, more desperate subject matter.

The girls played with the image of a boyfriend who would carefully choose the most perfect gift, set up an air of expectation, and then follow through with an extraordinary moment. They all delighted to imagine that God was like this boyfriend, or that a boyfriend like this could actually exist.

We had recently heard a girl's story about the end of a romantic relationship. During that story, the girls had shared their common practice of never leaving a loved-one while still angry. In amazement, they all shared a commonly held, deep-seated belief that God punishes the particular "sin" of not asking forgiveness for expressing anger. Clearly, they all worried that leaving in anger would result in a punishment, particularly a tragedy leading to death or dismemberment. The result would be guilt and the inability to ever repair the relationship. While the girls could not name exactly where this belief and its accompanying practice *came from*, they were all clear that it functioned in their lives.

Over against a God who keeps tally of their infractions and doles out punishment in the guise of seemingly random life tragedies, these girls found in Jo's story a different image of God. This is a God who cherishes their uniqueness and looks for the opportunity to bestow a well-chosen gift.

In this story and our conversation around it, I saw souls expanding. While male imagery for the Holy still pervaded our talk, here God was free from the boxy confines of hurtful and abusive relationships.

Closed Boxes and Open Horizons

A second-hand Lane cedar hope chest sits at the foot of my marriage bed. My dad bought it at a yard sale, cleaned it up, and gave it to me for my seventeenth birthday. In it are no needlework doilies. I use it to store fragments of my education: notes from a university class on African American women's biographies, sermons from my first years of trying to preach what I learned in seminary, and a half-dozen notes of support from members of a white suburban church I helped lead through transition to a cross-racial clergy staff.

My hope chest is one of the thousands that rolled off the assembly line from the dawn of the twentieth century until August 2001, when the Lane Company's whistle last marked the change of round-the-clock shifts. Small white houses with front porches line up along the town's main streets, remnants of a time when men packed lunch pails and walked to work. During the 1940s and '50s, parents all over America purchased Lane cedar hope chests for their daughters as they got confirmed or graduated from high school. During World War II, advertisements in *Life* magazine and the *Saturday Evening* Post sold these heirlooms to servicemen who had them shipped to fiancées and girlfriends awaiting their return.[17]

Once gifted with a hope chest, young women were given handmade doilies, saved S&H green stamps to buy gravy boats, and collected other household items that would be stored away until after their wedding. An older woman I know described the hope chest as the

---

17. Information about the history of the Lane Cedar Hope Chest was gleaned from an exhibit at Avoca Museum, Altavista, Virginia.

"covered wagon" of the twentieth century. Like the covered wagon, the hope chest is a cultural icon calling to mind a tangible repository for a woman's hopes and dreams. As an icon, the hope chest represents traditional white Protestant virtues such as chastity before marriage, marriage as the primary marker of adulthood, and the value of delayed gratification.

These heirlooms remain the source of great pride among locals. Residents remember fondly that heyday, hoping to reinvent a similar niche in today's global economy. Buoyed by this heritage of civic optimism, the town is attempting to retool. Building on its remaining industrial base to recruit new high-tech jobs, it is seeking a new corner in the global market. One textile mill has retooled to make fiber optics and Kevlar fabric used to make bullet-proof vests worn by U.S. soldiers in Iraq. Workers are taking advantage of federal dollars to acquire retraining or are commuting to neighboring towns for work.

In the midst of this economic crisis, the girls who collaborated in this research project are also retooling. As they come of age in a town where everybody knows everybody's business and one does not have to look far to find common branches of the family tree, they expressed a desire, even a need, to expand notions of God if they are to find a spirituality to sustain them in adulthood.

What resources does the Christian faith bring to such white girls in a blue-collar town? A primary resource the Christian faith holds is the potential to offer safe, hospitable space where storytelling and theological reflection can take place. The girls relished the opportunity to name God and entertain nontraditional images of the divine. Adults who hope to foster healthy spirituality among adolescent girls can embrace this creative imagining.

Beyond this appropriate pastoral response, however, a more radical hope emerged from my listening to these hard stories. These girls helped me imagine a reconstructed church, a Christianity that brings God out of the cramped confines of an heirloom hope chest and into the fresh air of expanding horizons. Such a reconstructed Christianity would:

- name abuse where it exists. It would steadfastly support people like Cat, who confront the lingering evil of patriarchy within the church and a culture deeply shaped by damaging interpretations of Christianity.

- learn to unmask the invisible privileges that come with whiteness. It would find ways to break out of unjust systems that hamper all human potential and would prioritize anti-racist practices of hospitality, community, and global economics.

- define domestic spheres as places of nurture. It would honor the vocation of childhood and the right of children to live where violence has no room to flourish.

- teach boys and girls, women and men multiple ways of being masculine and feminine. It would reject cultural norms that teach boys to eschew emotion, hide from grief, and excuse violent outbursts. It would likewise create tolerance for girls who seek to speak the truths of their lives and reject the "tyranny of nice and kind."[18]

- befriend voices of difference. It would create alliances with people seeking emancipation from oppressive governments, social structures, and worldviews, finding co-laborers within other life-giving faith traditions.

This is a Christianity I fail to see lived out on a regular basis. Yet it is a vision of Christianity in keeping with the gospel, in keeping with much of Christian history and tradition, and desperately needed in the lives of the girls to whom I listened. It is a form of Christianity worth remembering, stretching toward, embracing, and celebrating when we find it.

---

18. Carol Gilligan and Lyn Mikel Brown, *Meeting at the Crossroads: Women's Psychology and Girls' Development* (New York: Ballantine Books, 1992), 41.

Chapter 6

"Okay with Who I Am"

Listening to Lesbian Young Women Talk about Their Spiritualities

PAT DAVIS

How does a young woman create or discover a relationship with God or the Holy when she's taught — by her family, or organized religion, or the culture, or all three — that she is unworthy? Many Christians adhere to the doctrine that until they are redeemed by God, they are sinful in God's eyes. Lesbian, gay, and transgendered youth are often taught that there is no redemption for them at all, that they are essentially "unsavable" and unacceptable because of their sexual orientations.

Gay or lesbian young adults often have very complex experiences of identity formation because of having to take into account how their identification as "homosexual" will impact their relationships with friends, families, present and future partners, and spiritual communities. They must also be aware of the social, political, and spiritual implications of living as lesbians and gay men in a heterosexual world. For many, it is only after all of these factors have been weighed that they can begin the process of identity formation, and "coming out" (or disclosure).[1]

---

1. A. R. D'Augelli, "Identity Development and Sexual Orientation: Toward a Model of Lesbian, Gay, and Bisexual Development," in *Human Diversity: Perspective on People in Context*, ed. E. J. Trickett, R. J. Watts, and D. Birman eds. (San Francisco: Jossey-Bass, 1994).

My identity formation as a high school teenager and young adult college student was not complicated by the social, political, and spiritual implications of my sexuality. As a European American heterosexual middle-class female, I grew up in the "North" — in Illinois and Indiana — where I was also an undergraduate student. Like the young women in this study, "my experience of refining my spirituality involved my relationships to family, friends, and church, my sexuality, my body, and my psyche, along with my thinking about and relationship to God."[2]

My interest in and passion for the subject of lesbian spirituality arises from a debt of gratitude to teachers, members of my family, and caregivers who loved women, and who supported, encouraged, and nurtured me from my earliest years. And it arises from the debt of love I owe to my daughter, Sarah, who inspires me daily with her wisdom, courage, love, and optimism that things can and will be better. My interest also arises from the debt I owe my lesbian friends who have shared their journeys with me — in spirituality groups, in invitations to their sacred unions, in walks, and talks, and laughter.

This is a very small study, consisting of interviews with three young women — Sandra, LaToya, and Keva — who are self-identified as lesbians, and who are students at a private denominational university in the South. The aim of the study was very general: namely, to begin to hear the voices of lesbian young women talking about their experiences of spirituality in light of their sexual orientation.[3] Horror stories abound of young people who "come out" to their families and religious communities, only to be shunned, turned away, or even physically harmed.

---

2. Patricia Davis, *Beyond Nice: The Spiritual Wisdom of Adolescent Girls* (Minneapolis: Fortress Press, 2001), 11.

3. Although all three of these young women identified spirituality as an important part of their emotional and psychological lives, spirituality continues to be an understudied topic in literature on youth and in literature on gay and lesbian persons in general. This is striking, considering that some of the major underpinnings of political opposition to gay and lesbian rights across the board is based in the religious doctrine propounded by conservative Christians.

In a 1990 study of five hundred young lesbians, gay men, and bisexual men and women who sought the support of a New York facility for sexual minority youth, it was found that almost half had experienced some kind of violence related to their sexual orientations. A startling 61 percent of those who had experienced an assault experienced it within their families.[4] A similar 1995 study of almost two hundred sexual minority youth found that 22 percent of the young women had been verbally abused and 18 percent had been physically assaulted by members of their own families.[5] One recent study of gay, lesbian, and bisexual youth found that 42 percent of their sample of almost two hundred had attempted suicide on at least one occasion as the result of being victimized by or alienated from family, peers, or other community members.[6]

Although none of the three women I interviewed identified any physical abuse as the result of their sexual orientations, all three identified rejection by and struggles with family and their religious communities. The three come from very different religious backgrounds: Sandra was Roman Catholic and is now Wiccan; LaToya is Baptist; Keva's family attended a Methodist church and a "Bible church." All three were obviously initially devastated by the pain of being rejected and especially being rejected by their families. All three identified struggles with parents based on religious doctrine.

Four themes emerged strongly from the young women's interviews:

1. All three discussed being willing to hide their sexual orientations for the sake of harmony and good relationships in their families or religious communities.

---

4. Joyce Hunter, "Violence against Lesbian and Gay Male Youths," *Journal of Interpersonal Violence* 5 (1990): 295–300.

5. N. W. Pilkington and A. R. D'Augelli, "Victimization of Lesbian, Gay and Bisexual Youth in Community Settings," *Journal of Community Psychology* 23 (1995): 33–56.

6. S. L. Hershberger and A. R. D'Augelli, "The Impact of Victimization on the Mental Health and Suicidality of Lesbian, Gay, and Bisexual Youths," *Developmental Psychology* 31, no. 1 (1995): 65–74.

2. All three discussed struggling with the implications of their sexual identities for their past and future lives and relationships.

3. All three had creatively revised their own beliefs about God in order to maintain their spiritualities. Sandra decided to join a religious community that valued her and was more congenial to her beliefs; LaToya discovered biblical criticism and through it distanced herself from the intense criticism of her family and church; Keva, while still in some sense in the thrall of religious intolerance, also has begun to transform criticism into art.

4. Family members, especially mothers, were also sometimes examples of strength, inspiring the young women to assert themselves as faithful people and as lesbians.

So hear these young women's stories as narratives of courage in the face of conflict, struggle, and alienation. Also, hear them as the stories of young women who are defining new ways of being in relationship with God, their families, and their faith communities.

Sandra

The faith of my family is still a very integral part
of my religious life.

In order to find young women to interview for this project I had sent out an alert to several women who work with women students both in and outside the classroom. At least three women from three different organizations called me immediately, and recommended Sandra's name. "She is incredible." "She is so full of energy." "She is a person you *must* interview."

It took two weeks to schedule an hour with her, for in addition to keeping a near 4.0 grade point average, she also has a part-time job, works with the Women's Center, organizes events for PATH — the Wiccan student organization she founded on campus — and was

organizing a Halloween party for gay, lesbian, bisexual, and transgendered students on campus. The day I met with her, she had been
"testing" her costume for that party — a puffy red Pirate shirt, black
pants, and dramatic black makeup — and hadn't had time to change.
A very dramatic introduction to a very dramatic young woman!

Sandra began the interview by talking about what she believes is
the "most interesting thing" about herself:

> The most interesting thing? Well, kind of a two-part question,
> because the most interesting thing about me is "Hello? I'm a
> witch." So that usually — people go "Ohh. Really, now?" Um,
> so . . . and, I'm also Latina.

Sandra's spirituality and her activism for Wicca on campus was no
doubt one of the reasons she was so admired by many of the women
who referred me to interview subjects for this project and has been
the topic of much controversy and discussion on her campus. She
relishes the victory inherent in her founding of a pagan group at a
denominational university:

> To our knowledge, PATH is the first student organization of its
> kind at [this denomination's] schools. Of course, there are other
> ones in every public university these days — they all have at
> least one pagan or Wiccan group. But PATH is the first in this
> denomination's schools. Which is really cool.

She first encountered Wicca as the end of a search for how to put
her most basic beliefs together in a meaningful way. She talks about
beginning with Catholicism, then exploring nondenominational Christianity, and finally finding Wicca on the Internet and realizing that it
expressed her beliefs:

> So I took the overwhelming part of [my beliefs] and I really
> thought about what it meant and what place that held. . . . I went
> to the Internet. I found from that point some Internet sites that
> were talking about their experience with Wicca, with different

pagan religions. And I found that imaginary "what I would do" if it were my perfect world. That a lot of the things I had thought of [aligned] with what these people were practicing. It was like "Hey! Here it is! I thought I was coming up with something completely new, and here it is that people have actually written books about this."

Sandra freely admits, however, that her spiritual activism and non-traditional beliefs had their roots deep in the spiritual openness of her parents' progressive and Jesuit-influenced Catholicism:

My spirituality is kind of a little of both [paganism and Catholicism]. It was...the story of my life: I was raised in a Catholic family that was very conducive to questioning faith, actively teaching the faith, and discerning what that means and how you're going to live that in your life. So...and my parents hang out with the Jesuits way too much. (laughs)

An important part of the legacy of her parents' religion for her was their willingness to go out of their way, to make extra effort, and to challenge local authority in order to be part of a religious community in which they could worship with integrity. Her parents switched dioceses and became a part of a fledgling community in order to be with people who could tolerate and accept their questions:

At that time we had moved to Colorado. And at the time that bishop and the diocese of Denver were a little more conservative than my parents liked. So actually we would go to Catholic Mass in a different diocese. We'd drive all the way out — I don't know which one — where this small group were starting their own church. They hadn't gotten a building yet, but they were meeting at a school gymnasium and having Jesuits from a local retreat house come to say Mass. Which, I mean, and that's the tone of what real spirituality and real religious life ought to be like, in my mind.

Just as her parents were not afraid to be critical of their religious communities, Sandra does not accept the "orthodoxies" of Wicca uncritically, but rather draws her authority from her own experience:

> Some big national hoity-toity [Wiccan] group will say, "Oh yeah, we've done this for centuries, and that's where we get our authority from. . . . " If they draw authority from that, that's fine. I don't need to. I have lost connection with what my ancient ancestors did, you know. . . . I draw my authority from what I know to be true. My experience. Which is, you know, from a pagan point of view that's very like, "Well DU-uh!" Because pagan religions are all very experiential. It's "What is your experience, and what calls to you?"

For Sandra, leaving the Catholic faith was not a snap decision. She states that it took a long time. In the end, she wanted a faith community in which personal relationships were paramount, and in which others would call her personally to ethical accountability for her actions. She relates: "I wanted accountability, and I wanted more than just a watchdog group to force me to act my faith. But I also wanted kind of a religious culture where that was the norm. Where people just expected that of you. And expected you to be personally involved." She also wanted to be part of a community in which she could personally act as a woman, as opposed to having others act for her:

> I didn't want to be watching my religion being enacted by someone who was divinely ordained to be better than me at enacting my faith. I wanted to be acting my faith, which is something you find in pagan religion in general.

She is very proud that her parents support her in her Wiccan beliefs, and she sees traces of their faith in her own.

> I don't see disparity between what I believed growing up and what I was taught to believe, and what I believe now. I see it

very much as natural growth and progression of my faith life. And in many ways my parents agree. I sit down with my mom, and she'll say, "Oh, Sandra, you'd make such a good Catholic! These are all things I believe as a Catholic!" And I say, "Oh, Mom, you'd make such a good witch! You say all the things that witches believe!"

Despite what sounds like wistfulness in her mother's statement, when Sandra is challenged for her beliefs at school, her mother comes through for her. Notably, her mother has stood up for Sandra's controversial expression of her spirituality even when Sandra herself had tried to avoid "problems" with the theology teacher at her Catholic girls' school, for example, offering to hide a symbol of her faith (a pentacle) while she was in his class:

Junior year I started wearing a pentacle and had some problems with that. I had a couple of theology teachers who thought that it was very satanic, and you couldn't have any of that. And my mom actually stood up for me on that one. We had a theology teacher call the house one night after I had spoken with him in class that day. He called me aside and said, "What is this?"

And I said, "Oh, it's a symbol of my faith, here's what it means. I can take it off or tuck it in my blouse before I even come into your class. This doesn't have to be an issue." Okay, non-issue. . . . And in the back of my mind going, "I'm also gay, but we don't even want to go there!" He was like, "That's okay, no, that's fine, whatever. It's good that we had this talk." And then he called the house that night. Well, of course, my family got into this.

When the teacher called, Sandra had already prepared her mother, and she is very pleased that her mother listened to her account and then stood up for her:

So the call comes and the guy was like, "I'd like for you to know that your daughter is wearing a satanic symbol." And my mom looked straight at me, goes back to the phone, and goes, "No, she's not."

And the guy says, "Look at her closely. She might be wearing this necklace that has a star. . . . "

And my mom says, "Sir, that's a pentacle that's a sign of a faith. That has nothing to do with Satan."

And I feel like, "Way to go, Mom!" My mom is a teacher, but she knew — not at my school, but at another one — so she knew rules, faculty, she's got connections, she knows the principal, the administration. My family's in the know. So she goes, "You know, I don't know if you have permission to be calling here at my house this late at night. My daughter says you've already discussed this in school and that it's not an issue. Is it, in fact, a problem? Should we arrange a conference? You can call me at my business number."

The guy goes, "Well, ah, she — I don't know, she — " and hangs up, and my mom goes, "well that was great" and immediately picks up the phone and starts calling the principal, the administration. . . . "I'd like you to know that this teacher did this."

It was clear that Sandra learned a great lesson of faith that day — that her personal religious experience was worth standing up to "authorities" and engaging in conflict for, even with theology teachers. She also learned a wonderful lesson about her mother: that her mother would gladly, happily, and heartily champion her cause.

As difficult as it may have been, however, for her parents to accept Sandra as a witch, it appears that it was much more difficult for them to accept her lesbianism. Sandra talks about her coming out to them in a much less enthusiastic tone. According to her, she was not clear about exactly what she was doing when she first came out to them:

I was Wiccan before I came out. And when I came out, I didn't really have a sense of coming out. You know, now I . . . it was just a natural thing. It was just like, you know, I don't really remember hearing terms like "homosexual" or "lesbian" or things like that growing up. You know my family's very open about sexuality.... But I don't recall ever hearing about these things. And I went to a private, all-girls Catholic school for high school. So I know I didn't hear about it at *all* at school! So I don't know, it just...it was honestly before I even had words, before I had a language to talk about it, there was something I knew I was doing with my life.

By her junior year in high school she realized that she was not attracted to boys, and was not interested in dating them, as she had done to satisfy her parents in her first two years of high school. She talks about wondering about why she needed to go out with boys, when she was attracted to girls:

I wanted to take this girl to the movies, like on a date. And my parents said, "Like on a *what?*" And I was just like, "Those guys that Mom had me going out with, they just...[pause]...I'm just going to take this girl, okay? You know? And I'm excited about it. Does my hair look o.k.?"

According to her, their response to her was shock and disapproval. This confused her and alienated her. She couldn't understand how her parents, who championed her nonconformist religious beliefs, could be so disrespectful and misunderstanding of her of sexuality.

And they said, "Oh no no no. You're going to get on the phone and you're going to call this girl and tell her you're not going out."

She wondered what had happened to her liberal parents when it came to her sexuality:

And family was so vitally important to me. My parents at that time were already kind of "All right, so our daughter's doing this pagan thing, and we're kinda...." You know, they knew that I was nonconformist already, so they kinda knew that what I was doing religiously, the changes that were happening, that it was probably going to be okay. They were already working with me on that. So when this other thing came along, they were just like, "We don't know what to do with this." *So we did not speak to each other for a year.*

The misunderstanding and disapproval were so deep that a gulf of silence and painful alienation developed.

> I was in high school, between the latter half of my junior year and halfway through my senior year in high school ... there was this big, looming unspeakable that no one was sure what to say about it or where it was going or if it was true. And so, there wasn't a whole lot of talking.

Once again, Sandra was in a position of being something unacceptable — this time, however, she was unacceptable to the ones she loved and admired the most. Her strategy to avoid the pain and conflict inherent in the situation was the same with her parents as it had been with her theology teacher; just as she volunteered to hide her pentagram in theology class, she denied her sexuality in her family. Even though she was dating women, she denied it to her father:

> During this time, actually, once a month or so we'd be sitting at dinner and Dad would do something like, "Pass the peas. So Sandra, are you gay?" And I of course would say, "No, no." We did this whole year where we would not speak at all, but when we did speak, I would deny. Whatever we needed to keep peace, to not break apart this family that was so important to me.

During the year of silence, she turned to her brother and sister and her young women friends at school for support, for her paganism and for coming out as a lesbian. With them she experienced the connection between her sexuality and her spirituality for the first time:

> At the end of junior year my friends and I all went camping together. And that night we kind of sat around the fire. And someone said, "In the past year Sandra has, in fact, come out. So in case anyone missed it, or wasn't in the loop, now you know."

And we talked about a lot of things, and I got a reaffirmation from that group of girls that it was okay, that I was loved, that I'm obviously not going to hell, and that I didn't need to be condemned and that the problems I was having with my family, that was going to heal over time. It was really great.

Ultimately, Sandra's mother broke the silence between them — apparently recognizing that Sandra was in a time of crisis. The two began rebuilding their relationship, through awkward but sincere and honest conversation.

We didn't speak for a whole year, and then at the end, roughly, of that year, you know, I had been in relationships behind their backs. In and out, which is so hard. I didn't have a mom to cry with when someone broke my heart, you know. So at the end of that year, broken up with once again and kind of mourning over that, and then Mom was just like, "What is up? I'm your mom, I can sense these things." And so I was like, "Okay, fine. You want to go here? Sure, we'll go there. I'm gay. My girlfriend just broke up with me. It would have been our three-month anniversary." So crack! Cry.

The first thing my Mom said was "I'm sorry." It was less of the "I'm sorry you've been broken up with," and more of the "I'm sorry you're gay. I'm so sorry, because your life is going to be lonely and long and hard. And I'm your mom and I want to keep you from these things. . . . "

Sandra reflects that the worst pain came from losing her family:

I'm thinking, you know, it doesn't have to be that way. It's only going to be lonely and painful if I don't have the support of my family. Which is obviously very important to me.

So I just, you know, I reasserted that I was, in fact, gay. And the bulk of my parents' issues were religious. Because, you know, as soon as my mom was finished with this outpouring of "I'm frightened from a mother's perspective for what your life could be," she really had to sit down and say, "You know, I've been raised, and we are faithful people, we are spiritual sinners, and where we draw a lot of our understanding from is what the church teaches, and the Catholic Church teaches that we love you as our daughter, as a cherished person, but that we can't condone or accept and we can't love what you're saying you want to live. You know that I want you to have relationships and to have a partner and to have a life and a family like our family has been, but I have to morally understand that that is bad for you. It's bad for you as a person, it's bad for your soul, and it's unhealthy."

Ultimately, however, Sandra respects the struggle her parents went through regarding her sexuality. She understands that they had both religious/ethical issues and personal fears with which to contend before they could accept her:

And so they had to work through a lot of that. And, I mean we're talking like seven, eight years ago. So painfully they have worked through this to the point that a couple of months ago I got a call from my father, and he said, "You know, there's this group [the PFLAG of the church they attend], and they work on being a support network."

True to form, when her parents decided to support her, they did it in a big and public way, and in the context of worship. During a Mass to support the various ministries of the church:

. . . they called and they said, you know, that they had been asked as a family to carry the banner for the gay group. And they really wanted to do it.

Sandra has become philosophical about the pain of the year of silence and understands that it was, perhaps, a good time for her — to clarify and solidify her identity — and for her parents — to decide which was more important, their beliefs or their daughter.

And so, you know the silence helped me as much as it helped them to calm down and prioritize. And to question myself, make sure that I knew what I was doing. Or at least . . . you rarely ever really know what you're doing. But just to figure out the path you're on. One thing I figure during that time was that there was no rush. There really wasn't any rush. That I was going to be gay my whole life. So that meant my parents had a whole lifetime to come to terms with that. That I had spent . . . how old was I? — I'd spent sixteen years of my life becoming gay, living who I was and feeling that out and learning to not even question it.

But when I came out, it just was the way I was, and I'd spent all my life learning who I was and understanding that and not second-guessing that, and then to dump sixteen years of what I had learned onto them all at once, and expect them to all be at the same place at the same time? Of course not. So that really helped me.

I mean at the same time it was awful and painful and just horrible, but needed. Needed so that I could take a rest and realize that I have a lot of time. It didn't have to be right there right then. And then, you know, that good would come, life would go on. And the trust, you know, the trust in the love that we had as a family.

At this point the only person in her extended family who does not know that she is lesbian is her grandmother. The family as a whole has decided that it would not be a good thing to tell her. This is painful for Sandra, but she is philosophical about this also:

It's painful that my grandmother doesn't know — like there's a piece of me she won't know. On the other hand, there are lots of pieces of me that she doesn't know. Lots of little trivial things. This is a pretty essential, pretty big thing. There's not really a place in her world where this would fit, you know. She's lived a full and wonderful life, and I don't need to make her entire life shift dramatically just so that I can fit my little piece into it.

I think she knows some of the truth inside. Some of those really important things. Not necessarily who I'm attracted to, but that I love people. That I love life, you know, and there are things I'm involved in. She doesn't need to know the details.

You know we only have so much time left, and I have so much respect for her. When I get around her there's nothing I want to say about myself. I just want to hear what she has to say. Whatever she wants to talk about, I just want to know what it is.

Sandra ends her interview where she begins, by discussing her need to remain silent about who she is in the face of a possible misunderstanding by an important family member. This time, her desire is to say "nothing" about herself—and to listen. She hopes, however, that her grandmother "knows some of the truth" inside—even if they are not able to talk about it.

LaToya

I thought it's "Come as You Are," and I just don't get it.
You know what I mean?

I met LaToya in my office in the early evening, after she had just finished a hard practice with the women's basketball team at the university. She was tired but seemed enthused to be talking about her life. Throughout the interview she arranged and rearranged an ice bag on her left knee; she was a point guard on her team and played hard during practice as well as during games. She was also one of the newest members of the team, having transferred to the university in the fall as a junior.

She was as striking looking as Sandra: short and compact; tough-looking with tattoos on both arms and one leg (a panther—because it's "strong," her mother's initials, and a basketball); hair in cornrows; wearing basketball sweats. She was obviously proud of her physical condition.

As we began to talk, she made it clear that her family, and particularly her grandmother, brother, and mother, are the ones who sustain and motivate her. Her mother, especially, supports her in all aspects of her life, including the spiritual, relational, and athletic. Until her adolescence, church had been a constant factor in her life:

> Okay. I grew up in the church ever since I was born; I mean regularly, I mean required. Wednesday prayer meetings, you know, everything. If something was happening at the church, me and my brother and my mom was there.

In her early adolescence, her mother and their minister had a conflict that briefly put an end to the family's regular church attendance and seemed to have put an end to LaToya's regular attendance for good:

> I stopped going at the age around twelve, like on a regular basis. ...My mom was actually a singer in the choir, and the preacher wanted her to do.... She wasn't shouting enough for him, or something... he wanted her to like faint, and like you know, all of that.

Her mother, like Sandra's mom, refused to act according to the expectations of a religious authority when doing so would have meant acting nonauthentically:

> And she didn't feel the spirit that way, so she was like, "I'm not going to do it because then I would be doing something fake." So he told her well, she should excuse herself from whatever was happening, and we just never went back after that.

Her mother's assertion of the importance of her integrity had a great impact on LaToya. Although the family attended a Baptist church, and although most of her friends had been baptized in early childhood, LaToya waited, at her mother's insistence, until she felt ready to "do it on her own":

Yeah, because all my friends, growing up were saying, "Why haven't you ever been baptized?" and I'm saying, "My mama wants me to do it on my own will." Everybody else was pushed into it, or maybe doing it when they were five. I mean when you're five, you really don't know what you're doing it for. But my mama wanted me and my brother to do it on our own. And that was good, I did it on my own.

When asked what it meant to her to wait, she stated that it was a sign she was a child of God, and that she was "with herself seriously":

It made me have my own relationship with God, and not go off other people's testimonies. I'm having my own, because I did it for myself and I did it by myself. I wasn't with any family member or nobody, and I think that was the first step of me having my own personal relationship with God.

After LaToya's mother's conflict with their preacher, the family returned to the mother's childhood church. Her mother was much less involved there than she had been at their previous church. LaToya thinks it was because she knew fewer people and didn't feel as welcome. At the new church, LaToya became even less interested in attending worship. She began to feel that people (including her grandmother) who were being nice to her didn't really approve of her, especially with regard to her sexuality and the way she dressed:

I've known I was gay since I started going to school and knowing the difference between boys and girls. I was attracted to girls. I never liked boys. I always liked playing with boys, but when it came down to that part of it, no.

For her, the issue of clothes and the way she dressed came to symbolize her sexuality and all the issues surrounding it. She wanted to dress in pants, but that was not acceptable to her grandmother or the people of the church. She understands her church's rejection of her style of dressing to be a sign that she can't reveal her life to the congregation.

Even my Grandmama will be like, "You can't wear this to church, You can't wear this to church." But I thought it's "Come as You Are," and I just don't get it. You know what I mean?...If people are talking about simply clothes, you know, I'm pretty sure they're talking about everything else, too....My heart is as lonely as it's ever been. I keep my life close, like real close....I mean everybody talks about me like, "Why's she gonna want to...." Especially people who know me. People who know me know that I'm gay, and I bet they're saying, like, "Why is she coming to church?"

Although she questions whether she is being "paranoid," she feels that when she does come to church, the pastor seems to shift the topic of the sermon toward her and her sexuality:

That's the way I feel. I feel like he could have a sermon on anything, but as soon as I walk in, he'll change, or they have to mention it, anyway. You know, just mention it somewhere along the line....Like, this preacher right here loves to say that God didn't make Adam and Steve. And I'm like, "Are you kidding me?" I heard that when I was four. Are you serious? Change the name like Adam and Andrew. But you know, I mean... every time.

She states that it used to hurt her to hear these things from the pulpit when she was younger, to the point that she seriously questioned God about the fairness and reason of her being "born" gay: "When I was little, I was...I lied to myself. I put on a front. So whenever the pastor would say something, I felt like it didn't, you know, bother me." And, in addition to the religious pressure, she felt social pressure at school to be with boys and to appear more feminine:

You know you start going to school. "Why you don't have a boyfriend?" "Why are you dressed like your brother?" "Why don't you wear any makeup?" "Why you don't want to wear a skirt?..." And I wasn't comfortable with myself at the time, so that would have been a bad time. But now it doesn't matter. Right. But back then, just walking on eggshells, keeping all that in, and putting on a front.

All of this — the religious and social pressure — affected her feelings about God:

> I was really bitter toward God in my younger ages, because I didn't understand why...I would always say, "Why me?"...My family, well we assumed one of my aunties was, but no one ever talked about it. And when you're young and you know that's how you are and you don't have nobody to talk to, so it's kinda like you're by yourself. And you just think about it. The stuff builds up, and you kinda...I just always ask Why why why why why why?
>
> I did this. I prayed about it ever since my mama taught me how to pray. But when I was five and up, it was like maybe you're not believing in your heart strong enough. Well, I did. Because I wanted to be like my other girl cousins. I wanted to, you know, yeah, I wanted to feel comfortable in a dress and just go out and chase boys. I wanted to do all that, but it never came to me like that. I did not want to do it. I wanted to play some ball and do everything that my brother did. Or my other boy cousins. I didn't want to play Strawberry Shortcake.

Her current attitude toward the preacher is resignation: She wearily states:

> It's sort of funny to me now. But when they say it now, you know, I don't say nothing.

Interviewer: But how does it make you feel to hear that?

> You know, you expect to hear it now, so it's not a big deal.

It's clear that LaToya draws on the strength of her baptism experience and the example of her mother in her response to her preacher's harassment. She doesn't hesitate to criticize him; nor does she hesitate to believe that he is wrong about her: "I don't think he's telling the complete truth, no, I don't. So I don't...Not when it comes to my spirituality, I don't think so."

She is also very clear in her own mind that the Bible is wrong about her sexuality. This assurance came out of a preparatory class for baptism, in which she used her own judgment to label what she found to be a clear error in scripture regarding slavery:

> In some parts of the Bible it's like, um, I don't know who wrote this part, but it was like, "The slave should obey thy master." And I don't believe that because I don't believe there should be a slave or a master. So I didn't believe in that. I don't believe it, the homosexual part of it. So some things that I picked out I didn't believe in it.

By the time she went to college, she was ready to trust her own feelings about herself more completely. Her self-acceptance didn't come in a moment, but rather through a process of allowing herself to be critical of those who would "say something" about her:

> I was thinking one day that I couldn't live my life the way people wanted me to, especially if I didn't think nothing was wrong with it. And people are always going to have something to say about you. I just grew out of it.

In addition, at college, she was introduced to biblical criticism and came to an understanding of the Bible that allowed her to gain a perspective on the passages that her preacher had repeated against her:

> And I learned about that my sophomore year in college when I was nineteen. That's when I really came into my own. I was in this class, it was an English class. But it was like a theology building. You could either take English or that. It was a spirituality class, and we went over the Bible and everything, and our teacher was a Catholic, and he made us open up the Bible and he told us what was God actually saying. What was added or written in.

And he talked about the Q. His actual sayings and everything. Just put a lot of things in our minds and let us really think about it. And like a lot of people dropped out of the class because they thought it was wrong for you to even question it. That's how my grandmama is, though, question nothing about it. "It is what it is."

If I never went to that class, I probably would feel … no doubt in my mind I'd still do what I'm doing, but that God thinks it's wrong probably would still be in my mind and I would still have some … I wouldn't like myself like I do now.

Her Bible class has helped LaToya to relativize and diminish the impact of passages that might otherwise make her feel like "God thinks it's wrong" for her to "do what I'm doing." Like Sandra, LaToya has learned to trust her own individual experience of God.

Like Sandra, however, LaToya and her family have had a hard time coming to terms with her being lesbian. On the one hand, she believes her grandmother is accepting of her, because her grandmother has gay friends. On the other hand, LaToya knows that she wishes LaToya would dress differently. Their biggest problems seem to be related to church.

Her mother seems more accepting of her sexuality on one level, but also seems to think of LaToya's being lesbian as a defect — too many male hormones:

Well, my mama says if people can be born like, you know, Siamese twins and everything, why couldn't somebody be born, you know, having feelings for the same sex? That's just her way of thinking about it. I think she does mean in a defect way, because that maybe I have too many male hormones. And that's a defect, isn't it?

She had come out to her mother four years previously. She states that her mother felt betrayed that LaToya had not told her earlier. At the same time, LaToya didn't feel that her mother took her seriously enough at the beginning.

> I told her when I was fifteen. And that's how it was. But then when I told her that time, she said, "Oh, that's just a phase." So she kind of brushed it off. Then when it continued, you know, then she said, "Well, it's not a phase," you know, and "that's not right. You need to go more to church."

Nevertheless, when asked what she most wants people to remember her for she states it would be for her honesty.

> I hope the world knows me, but the people for sure will know me that honesty is the best policy. I'm always honest. And just to be yourself. And don't try to live your life through somebody else, and don't let somebody make you feel you should live your life for somebody.

> *Interviewer:* So for somebody who felt that she had some secrets in her early life, honesty is the best policy is quite a radical thing to say.

> Because I wish I would have told my mama, you know, earlier. It would have saved her from guessing and a lot of the arguments that we had.

Keva

*They are not hostile to me as a person,
just hostile toward my sexuality.*

I met Keva in my office just after dinnertime on a weeknight. She had brought a sandwich with her, but didn't eat during the interview — she seemed almost embarrassed by it. She carried a backpack that seemed almost larger than she was; it was overflowing with art supplies. Her very short hair was pitch-black and spiky. She wore multiple earrings in each ear, and silver bracelets on her wrists. In contrast to her dramatic appearance, however, she was extremely soft-spoken and introspective.

Keva has no brothers or sisters and considers herself very close to her parents. Both her mother and father currently live in a small town in east Texas. She talked about her spiritual background as being somewhat eclectic, due to her parents' divorce when she was in early elementary school:

> When I was very young we were Catholic, so we went to Mass every Sunday. Then my dad started going to the Methodist church, so then my mom switched over, and she went there until I was twelve or thirteen.... My parents divorced when I was seven. My dad started going to a Bible church and would take me sometimes. My mom and I kept going to the Methodist church. There were people in Dad's church who knew a lot about the Bible, and I started going to Bible study some when I got older. It was pretty conservative.

At the time she started attending these Bible studies she had already realized that she was gay. She talks about knowing that she was "different" in her feelings for girls, and waiting for crushes on boys to "kick in":

> I knew I was different as a child, but I was just somehow just really different. And I don't know what it was. But I never quite fit in, especially in junior high, like it was really obvious that I didn't fit in. I wasn't like other kids. And I always had crushes on girls, but I thought that was normal. I was like, "Oh," I just kept waiting for it to kick in, like with boys. Like, it'll come some day, I guess.

Her acceptance that she wasn't going to have feelings for boys seemed rather matter-of-fact:

> But finally it didn't, and then it was like, "Oh, okay. That's cool."
> I mean I didn't know what the word was, and I didn't really

associate the word "gay" for a long time, probably until I was fifteen or sixteen. And then for a while it got so weird.

But as with Sandra and LaToya, it engendered an intense fear of losing the love and respect of her parents:

> You know, you always hear the horror stories about if you come out with your parents. That to me was so frightening, because you know, all I had were my parents. It would be awful if I didn't fit in. And so finally when I was eighteen my mother, she said, you know, "Do you think you could be gay?" Because maybe you could have inherited it. It was very cool.

The Bible studies with her father had a lasting effect on her. Currently, in her junior year in college, she is involved in another very conservative Bible study, which she joined at the invitation of a woman she met in a photography class. She talks about feeling like she should attend the Bible study, because she's trying to have many different types of experiences in the world, and she shouldn't "shut" these people "out."

> I met the woman in my photography class, and we started talking and she asked me to go to a Bible Study, and I mean she is a really hard-core religious person. You know, I've been around people like that before, but at the same time I don't feel I should shut it out because maybe it's not necessarily anything that I believe. I can certainly be like, okay, this is not what I believe.

She talks about being impressed with how friendly the "kids" in the Bible study are to her, but also having the feeling that they might be spiritually superficial, and they might have an agenda for her:

> They're definitely really nice kids. Really nice people. Almost too friendly. So that makes me a little uncomfortable at times. And I mean it's interesting to go and listen to what many of these people have to say about the Bible and everything. Some of it I don't think they really think through. I don't necessarily see

everything they're saying. And maybe just because I would have been questioning it so much. But at the same time they act like they've believed it all their lives, not even questioning it.

One of the most remarkable aspects of this group, for Keva, is that the women accept the idea that they should be subordinate to men:

> I went to this one Bible study class, and they were talking about since Eve ate the apple first, it was woman's fault for sin. And that, you know, men are definitely supposed to rule over women. It didn't make any sense that, you know, women should submit to their husbands. And that women have to know that they have influence over their husbands, so they have to be careful about how they influence their husbands, because their husbands didn't make the best decisions. I think at one point this girl said, "You know the greatest position I could ever hold would be a mother, because I'd know I had so much influence." And I said why wouldn't she want to be the president, because wouldn't she have so much more influential power? That doesn't make any sense.

Hearing them talk about women being subordinate made Keva suspicious that they would also have "biblical" views about homosexuality:

> It's hard to relate with this kind of person because they're so into, like, this is what the Bible says and this is how it should be. And especially for a homosexual going in and knowing, "okay, that there are passages in the Bible where it says this, this, and this." And I have my own philosophies on how to interpret that. Because there are a lot of different ways. But you know, these people know just the way it is supposed to be.

She took the initiative to talk with her friend about the issue, and her suspicions were confirmed: her friend told her that being gay was the "embodiment" of sinful human nature:

> She told me that this was my "choice" and that God didn't really want you to do it this way, that I should celebrate myself and the

idea of changing. And to me, it doesn't make any sense. I mean she was like, in a way it's an embodiment of man's sins, if man sinned in the past, man sins now. And that to me was a little overdone.

When asked how it made her feel to know how her friend felt, she seemed almost to excuse it, but also challenged the woman's assumptions about her choice in the matter:

Oh, well, you know I'm okay with who I am, and I feel so strongly about who I am, that it doesn't really matter. I can say, "Let's just agree to disagree." You know, that's not how I feel. And obviously you're not going to understand it because you haven't experienced it.... And I think she was caught off-guard one time, but she talked to me about — we were talking about love, and she said to me like, "Well, you have to try to love a man"... something like that. And I said, "I can't, and that's not going to happen. Do you think you could fall in love with a woman?" And she said, "Oh, wait, no. I couldn't do that, I mean, Oh. I mean it's just kinda 'oh, wait a minute.'" So I could get the impression that she doesn't really understand it, and she really doesn't have.... In some ways she can't understand just because she's in such a simplistic lifestyle.

Interviewer: It doesn't hurt you, though, to go there? It doesn't upset the way you think about yourself?

Yes, it does, but I mean, I'm so strong in my sexuality that it's not, it's not something that's ever going to change. And it's a part of me, it's not all of me. But I don't feel like it's wrong. They are not hostile to me as a person, just hostile toward my sexuality. And I'm so complete in that and so okay with that that that's all right... and it's interesting to hear them say, you know....

Her art, which she feels is the most important thing in her life, is intensely spiritual and filled with religious imagery.

I am painting a lot of mystical stuff, and I never would have thought of my art as being spiritual, but it is all about the presence of this other being, otherworldliness.

Her newest projects are self-portraits — which she sees as proof that she exists in the context of a world in which there is "something bigger than myself."

And particularly in photography I've been exploring a lot of self-portraits, so it's more of a symbol for me and a symbol for being or existing and more of a turning toward something bigger than myself. But you know in a lot of ways that's what art is for — that you should say something, or really point to a part of meaning, or some sort of universal truth.

In these photographs, however, a viewer can see what may be the results of her "education" by the members of the Bible studies she's attended. They are pictures of suffering — her own, and the entire gay community's — in relation to Christ's suffering:

And then, I just want to find more and more religious symbols. I tried to do one with a message, and it was an abstract photograph — but it was supposed to be about my being martyred on the cross. But it wasn't exactly me; it was the whole gay community. And there are just people that are looking and looking and looking. . . . You will be persecuted just like I was persecuted. And it doesn't matter who you are necessarily. And it could be for nothing and it could be so little of who you are, and you just get persecuted for that. So I just kinda thought that was an interesting idea. So I feel like you gotta be able to cry about it.

She spoke very briefly about trying to portray a sense of redemption in her work, but when asked who is redeemed by the picture of herself on a cross, she states that — in fact — she just feels stared at, and like hanging on the cross is the ultimate sacrifice of herself:

I don't know if there's any redemption, because it feels like these people are staring at me. It's really the "ultimate" me, just put up there and looked at from every angle because that's what people do to you. And that's what they do to lots of people. It's the sacrifice of myself, you know, it's so personal.

She realizes that, although she would like to be a full-time artist in the future, she may never have the amount of time she currently has to devote to her art. So, her goal for her time in college is to develop herself as an artist as much as she can. That includes trying to understand universal truths about the world:

This time can be about me. And so I guess I've been working, working, working, and really looking at my life and trying to become more universal, and trying to really get a grasp on things on a different level. I guess I want to say a more adult level, but it's something bigger than that. It's something more . . . I mean . . . I just feel that there's something new and exciting that really speaks to me about people and really wants me to examine that, and to come up with . . . maybe spiritual ideas that are supposed to be bigger than you . . . and a lot about suffering. It's kinda depressing though.

◆ ◆ ◆

It is impossible to generalize about lesbian young women's lives from such an extremely small sample of interviews. Nevertheless, their stories suggest that families and church communities that are mindful of the spiritual needs of lesbian youth need to be aware that *disapproval* of a young woman's sexual identity can be destructive of both her life and spirituality. For these three women, their sexual identities were obviously not something layered "on top" of all their other identities — their identity as lesbians is close to the core of their spiritualities.

For these young women, being cut off from parents, grandparents, and church communities was experienced as real and devastating — on occasion so devastating that they were willing to hide themselves in order to restore relationships. Sandra was willing to tell her father that she wasn't gay; LaToya tried to "lie to" herself about who she was when she heard her pastor condemning gays; Keva was very reluctant to "come out" to her parents for fear she would be rejected by them.

Although it is true that rejection of these young women's sexual identities can lead to great pain, it also seems to be true that support of their sexual identities can unleash huge forces of creative energy and inspiration. Two of the women talked about independent thinking and action on the part of their mothers, which gave them the example and courage to reject the "orthodoxies" of their early religious communities. Sandra became a witch — even while attending a Catholic girls' school; LaToya waited to be baptized until she felt ready, at her mother's insistence, and currently does not attend church regularly because she feels oppressed by the preaching and by church members who she is sure talk disapprovingly of her when she is not present.

None of the young women described a religious community in which they felt completely comfortable — even now. Sandra struggles with some of the orthodoxies of the Wiccan religion — and accepts only what she can confirm by her own experience. LaToya has found a comfortable understanding of the Bible, based on biblical criticism that helped her to distance herself from rigid interpretations of verses regarding homosexuality. But that understanding has distanced her from her faith community and her grandmother. Keva attends a Bible study that continues to be hostile toward her sexuality, and creates art depicting herself and the entire gay community as suffering on a cross — stared at humiliatingly by the rest of humanity.

The story of sexual minority youth and their experiences of spirituality is only beginning to be told, as they are beginning to step forward. Telling their experiences is a courageous act in itself — in a religious context that is, for the most part, anything but accepting. As we listen, those of us who are in the majority sexual community will need to be willing to face our own complicity in hurting and alienating these women. And we will need to protect them, insofar as we are able, from the abuse they may experience as the result of sharing their experiences with us.

In listening, we will need to be prepared to journey into their great pain and doubt. But we will also be enriched — by stories of faith, refusal to give up hope, and steadfast love and commitment in the face of hostility. In short, the stories of these young people are the stories of the gospel, being lived out and spoken to us in this generation. We must have ears to hear.

Conclusion

Nurturing the Sacred Selves of Adolescent Girls

EVELYN L. PARKER

We will dance through the gates of heaven and be at peace.
— Kateri Quoetone, Kim and Pam Ahhaitty

The quotation above, from the poem "Feathers of the Wind: Our Footsteps as Kiowa Young Ladies," which we encountered earlier in this book, offers beautiful imagery of joy and peace upon arriving in heaven that is unparalleled by any earthly experience of Kateri, Kim, and Pam. In their poem they express their anticipated celestial ecstasy in the bodily movement of dancing. In the introduction I wrote about observing the embodied expression of Kim's spirituality during her performance of the Honor Dance at the Pueblo Pow Wow in Taos, New Mexico.

Dancing, and the spirituality it expresses, is clearly very important to the Kiowa Nation as it is also to other Native American peoples. In addition to the Honor Dance, performed on the occasion of grand marches and other formal events, the Sun Dance, Ghost Dance, and Gourd Dance continue to be common among the people of the Kiowa Nation and other American Indians of the Plains and Prairies. The Sun Dance, in which dancers circle a sacred tree or pole and stare at the sun, is a purifying ritual that seeks to bring peace to lost relatives. The Ghost Dance commemorates a time of flourishing on the plains when the land was full of buffalo and devoid

161

of white people.[1] The Gourd Dance, originally a victory dance of Kiowa warriors, has become central to the Pan-Indian cultural revitalization movement.[2] In 1883 the U.S. government criminalized the Sun Dance and many other dances of Native Americans.[3] Guy Quoetone, the great grandfather of Kateri, Pam, and Kim, was forbidden to dance while attending the J. J. Methvin Methodist Institute, a boarding school near Anadarko, Oklahoma, because of the government ordinance aimed at enculturation.[4] Despite these harsh institutional and governmental policies, Guy Quoetone, along with members of his family, passed on traditional dances to Kateri, Pam, and Kim. When the girls dance we see the essence of their spirituality, that is rooted in the culture of the Kiowa Nation and nuanced by the Methodist religious tradition.

Throughout history, dance has been an expression of the dancer's deep relationship with creation, humankind, and the Divine. In tribal communities, like the Kiowa Nation, dance is the means by which joy, sadness, love, and hate are expressed, the stages of life are celebrated, and resistance and power are expressed.[5] The Kogi Indians of South America practice a "divine dance" that completes the life cycle of one who died too soon. The Kogi ritual dance has three major movements. The community remembers, in the first movement, "by becoming entangled in the threads of the person's shroud and then unraveling these threads." Second, the community envisions new ways of being in relationship with their beloved deceased and with each other "as the people search for and gather the appropriate songs from among the community with the aid of a priestly leader." Last of all, the community

1. Joel W. Martin, *The Land Looks after Us: A History of Native American Religion* (New York: Oxford University Press, 1999), 92–93.

2. C. Ellison, "Truly Dancing Their Own Way: Modern Revival and Diffusion of the Gourd Dance," *American Indian Quarterly* 14, no. 1 (Winter 1990): 19–35.

3. Martin, *The Land Looks After Us*, 93.

4. Clyde Ellis, "Boarding School Life at the Kiowa-Comanche Agency, 1893–1920," *Historian* 58, no. 4 (Summer 1996): 777–94.

5. Lynn Frances, "Sacred Dance and Spirituality." See *www.hartcentre.demon.co.uk/scithrev.htm*.

reweaves "through the singing and dancing of these songs, the threads of connection in a richer and more complex symbolic pattern."[6]

Dance has been practiced by people of faith and has always been integral to liturgy and worship. David danced before the Lord joyously as the ark of God was brought from the house of Obededom (2 Sam. 6:14). Jephthah's unnamed daughter greeted him with timbrels and dancing upon his return from battle (Judg. 11:34). The writer of Psalms 30:11 reminds us that mourning can be transformed into dancing. Dance expresses deep sorrow as well as sheer joy. Psalms 149 and 150 affirm dance as an appropriate way to "Praise the Lord!" in worship. Hebrew Bible scholar Walter Brueggemann indicates that singing and dancing among a select group of Israelite women was a common practice. These women were especially skilled in the singing and dancing required by the community in times of grief and death, as we see in Jeremiah 9:17 and 2 Chronicles 35:25, as well as times of joy, liberation, and victory, as we see in 1 Samuel 18:7.[7] Dancing and singing among Israelite women and girls provided a liturgical event in the life of the community.

I propose that dancing is therefore a fitting image for a wholesome spirituality in adolescent females amid the toxic social terrain of racism, sexism, classism, and heterosexism in North American society. This image reflects the epistemological and ontological aspects of a girl's spirituality, where her ways of knowing and being in the world are shaped by her beliefs in God and the practices of justice that she manifests. Her piety and her just practices are indistinguishable, just as a modern dancer's spine roll used during her warm-up is indistinguishable as a separate entity when part of a fluid performance. Dancing signifies a spirituality that offers a liberative hope to adolescent girls, a spirituality through which they view themselves as agents of God

---

6. Martha A. Robbins, "The Divine Dance: Partners in Remembering, Revisioning, and Reweaving," *Journal of Pastoral Care* 51, no. 3 (1997): 337–38.

7. Walter Brueggemann, "The Book of Exodus: Introduction, Commentary, and Reflections," in Leander E. Keck, convener, *The New Interpreter's Bible* (Nashville: Abingdon Press, 1994).

dismantling the systems and powers of injustice, moved by the convic-
tion that God is with them in spirit as they act. This is emancipatory
hope, a constructive response to the evil forces in society that marginalize girls who are different because of their race, class, social status,
gender, or sexual orientation.[8] Also, dancing is a dynamic image in
which embodied knowledge is central. Whether in exceeding joy or
great sadness, the spirit of a girl is set free when she dances.

Speaking of a girl's spirituality as dancing resonates with Maria Harris's idea in *Dance of the Spirit: The Seven Steps of Women's Spirituality*.
In this book she presents a woman's spirituality as a series of movements that nurture the soul, the private or inner life of a woman. The
steps are as practical as they are theoretical. They include the spiritual
disciplines and other practices compatible with the seven movements.
The indwelling Holy Spirit is the partner of the woman who engages
in the "dance of the Spirit."[9] While a focus on nurturing the inner
life of a woman is one important aspect of her spirituality, a constant
theme in the lives of the young women in this volume centered on
relationships that "affirm who she is becoming."[10]

Understanding a healthy spirituality of a girl in this way requires
that we focus on wholesome relationships with God, with significant
others, with those in her immediate communities (school, church,
peers), with those beyond, and with creation. The starting point for this
volume, unlike that of Harris, is the hard stories of girls that reveal
their struggles against oppression. A girl's effort against domination
and dehumanization is a dance of the spirit. It is an epistemological
and ontological stance, by which a girl's knowing and being provides a
hermeneutical lens and organic practice of consciousness, opposition,
tenacity, and fortitude. As Harris suggests, the indwelling Holy Spirit

---

8. Evelyn L. Parker, *Trouble Don't Last Always: Emancipatory Hope among African American Adolescents* (Cleveland: Pilgrim Press, 2003), 5.

9. Maria Harris, *Dance of the Spirit: The Seven Steps of Women's Spirituality* (New York: Bantam Books, 1989).

10. Patricia Davis, *Beyond Nice: The Spiritual Wisdom of Adolescent Girls* (Minneapolis: Fortress Press, 2001), 3.

is a girl's dance partner. However, the Holy Spirit is also the choreographer of the dance of life for a girl on the margins. God, the Holy Spirit, advocates on her behalf, reveals truth, helps her become aware, and is the Power that will transform her troubles.

If dancing is a dynamic image of a girl's spirit soaring to the heights of ecstasy and peace while coping with the sorrow and pain of marginalization, how might congregations nurture a wholesome spirituality among girls when they are bombarded by dehumanizing acts of racism, sexism, classism, and heterosexism? What are the essential elements for nurturing the spirituality of marginalized adolescent girls? How do the stories of the girls in this book inform our ministry with them? What biblical, theological, and educational resources can inform our practices of ministry with girls on the margins of society? Who are their partners along this journey?

A response to these questions suggests that pastors foster spirituality in girls so that they can dance in the abundance of life that only God through the power of the Holy Spirit provides. There are four essential components for congregations concerned with nurturing a wholesome and holistic spirituality in adolescent girls. These essentials are realization, resistance, resilience, and ritual. There is a theological significance in each of these four essentials that informs an *emancipatory* ministry with girls and the practices they manifest. I follow a discussion of each component and suggested practices with a midrashic reading of Miriam's story which serves as a poetic conclusion to each component. The life of Miriam, the sister of Aaron and Moses, the prophet who led the women in dancing and singing following God's act of the liberation of the Israelites from the Egyptians, brings the idea of girls' dancing as spiritual selfhood into focus.

Realization

A wholesome spirituality in adolescent females begins with the capacity for critical consciousness or critical thinking. In any given situation, a girl should be empowered to sense when she is being treated unjustly due to her race/ethnicity, gender, class, or sexual orientation. She should be able not only to respond from a gut level, but to have the capacity to name the problem in its systemic form. Girls should realize when something has gone awry and be able to name the wrongdoing on the basis of an understanding of systems and powers rather than merely personalizing the wrongdoing. Girls who choose to desecrate their bodies in order to mirror the cultural norm of "beauty" need to realize that their own beauty is normative. Girls who yearn for acceptance in their communities need to recognize the sociohistorical events and social policies that perpetuate internalized racism and classism. Girls who desire caring relationships with significant men in their lives need to understand the patriarchal ethos in their communities, the church, and the larger society.

The capacity for realizing what is problematic and developing critical consciousness about it as well is not a new idea. Many educators have written about critical consciousness and critical thinking, particularly Paulo Freire in his seminal book *Pedagogy of the Oppressed*. Many educators concerned about the formation of the Christian faith have appropriated his tenets. Few, however, have argued specifically that critical consciousness is an aspect of a healthy spirituality. Critical thinking and spirituality are wed in the girl who recognizes the presence of power and principalities at work in perpetuating poverty, denying opportunities due to sexual orientation, and silencing on the basis of gender. Realization is a girls' spiritual awareness of her own existential realities and those of her immediate and global community.

Maria Harris discusses awakening as a coming to awareness of the capacities and possibilities within one's self that constitute the first step of living out a woman's spirituality. This form of awareness is a personal and internal reflection on one's inner life and the promise that life holds. I am speaking of a different type of awareness that does not begin with the self as such but starts with observations of others and how they distort right relationships. This form of awareness presupposes an internal awareness that a girl knows she is created in the image of God and therefore has divine capacity to fulfill her human potential. The pivotal point of awareness is when a girl realizes that the image of God that she embodies has been affronted or violated.

The realization that I speak of is more akin to Maria Harris's idea of questioning found in her seventh step, that is, transforming. For Harris the transforming process involves a woman's care for the world so that humankind and creation are renewed/reborn. The rhythms move through listening, questioning, mourning, and finally to birthing. The second rhythm, questioning, is the voice that emerges from listening and asks who, what, and why questions about power relationships. The practice of questioning, which has purified and preserved Judaism and Christianity, is essential for transformation.[11]

Daring to ask questions is central to a girl's spirituality. Likewise, in critical theological questioning, girls "test the spirits" of culture.[12] In his discussion about the role of understanding in discernment, David White's idea of loving God with your mind comes closest to my idea of realization. He writes: "While the heart may be a primary way of knowing God and neighbor, the mind was for Jesus and is for us important for understanding the world's distortions and seeking ways to extend love more completely into the world, to heal its wounds."[13] For an adolescent girl, realization is loving God by the way she puts things together, how she makes sense of her discrete experiences and endows them with meaning.[14]

Practicing Realization with Girls

Helping girls to become aware of injustice in society and coaching them with critical thinking skills is the practical task of realization. Critical theological questioning with girls "means raising questions about the social and personal dynamics as shaped by economic, political, and

11. Harris, *Dance of the Spirit*, 179–87.
12. David White, *Practicing Discernment with Youth: A Transformative Youth Ministry Approach* (Cleveland: Pilgrim Press, 2005), 54.
13. Ibid., 120.
14. Ibid., 121.

cultural forces. . . . The appropriate questions are 'But why?' 'What are the reasons that this situation has emerged in history?' 'What are all of the influences upon this situation?' "[15] David White describes in detail several methods that can be appropriated as practices of realization with girls. Among these are the "But why?" method and exercises from the Brazilian activist and performer Agusto Boal.[16]

Two resources to help girls practice critical theological questioning are movies and newspaper or magazine articles about girls. These forms of popular culture are familiar to girls and provide opportunity for rich in-depth discussions. Develop a Faith, Film, and the Female/Feminine series. Invite junior high and senior high school girls to compile a list of movies in which a girl is the protagonist or the movie features girls. My list would include *Saved, Rabbit Proof Fence, Whale Rider, Mona Lisa Smiles, Thirteen, Bring It On I and II,* and *Mean Girls.* After showing the movie to the girls facilitate the discussion with questions that:

1. Help girls realize how females are represented in the movie.

   - How are the main characters portrayed?
   - What are the obvious stereotypes?
   - How do these characterizations compare with parallel characters in other movies?

2. Help girls become aware of the ways that females are on the margin or in the center of community and social interaction.

   - Who is popular? Who is not? Why?
   - Who is silenced? Who is given voice?
   - How and why are some girls silenced and some given voice?

3. Help girls become conscious about the marketing of the movie.

   - Why are the movie producers selling you this movie? What is for sale? What are you buying?

15. Ibid., 125.
16. Ibid., 127–29.

4. Help girls realize the biblical and theological implications of the movie.

- ◆ Is there a savior in the movie? If so, who is she or he and why is that character a savior?
- ◆ Is the image of the savior one you embrace? Reject? Why?
- ◆ What Bible passages come to mind from watching this movie?
- ◆ What is the nature of relationships in the movie?
- ◆ How are the relationships life-giving or wholesome? How are they not?
- ◆ If you could rewrite the movie script, what would it look like so that all the girls would flourish? What would abundant life look like?

Such a Faith, Film, and the Female/Feminine series is one method that can help girls practice realization through critical theological questioning. There are other creative methods that girls and their adult partners or facilitators can use to hone this aspect of girls' spirituality.

Realizing with Miriam

Miriam, the big sister of Moses, was smart, watchful, and wise. In silence she stood near the river's bank and watched her baby brother floating in a waterproofed papyrus basket. It was the plan of Miriam and her mother, Jochebed, that his clandestine voyage would not be noticed.

His sister stood at a distance, to see what would happen to him. (Exod. 2:4)

"From afar, not yet approaching the water itself, [Miriam] waits to know what will happen."[17] With an eagle's eye she watches intensely. Does she know she will shape the destiny of her brother and the history

---

17. Phyllis Trible, "Bring Miriam Out of the Shadows," in *Bible Review* (February 1989): 16.

of her people? When Pharaoh's daughter discovers the baby boy among the reeds, Miriam's questioning eye and critical mind empower her to speak:

> ...Shall I go and get you a nurse from the Hebrew women to nurse the child for you? (Exod. 2:7)

Pharaoh's daughter replies an emphatic "Yes," and Miriam goes and calls her mother, the mother of Moses. Jochebed nurses Miriam's baby brother until he grows up and is ready to be returned to Pharaoh's daughter. Miriam, the big sister of Moses, was smart, watchful, and wise.

Resistance

A healthy spirituality for a girl is one that resists those powers that seek to dehumanize her. Resistance is spiritual opposition to all that hinders the complete flowering of a girl. An oppositional spirit rejects the academic mediocrity of lazy school counselors and teachers and chooses academic excellence instead. With such a spirit a girl makes the basketball, soccer, and baseball teams despite the naysayers that question her athletic ability. An oppositional spirit will defy the stereotypical female role and become whatever she dreams: the engineer, the astronaut, the physician, the veterinarian, or the professional billiard ball player. Ebony, a teenage rapper, offers a fitting declaration of resistance when she writes: "My greatest hope is to be an inspiration to other females who wish to defy the limitations and stereotypes placed on their lives by society."[18]

Other types of injustice call for resistance. It is this that Maria Harris discusses as the third step of "Formgiving" in the "Creating Movement." In situations of injustice and evil "someone must resist, even rebel, against that situation."[19] Resisters are those who accept

18. Hillary Carlip, *Girl Power: Young Women Speak Out!* (New York: Warner Books, 1995), 210.
19. Harris, *Dance of the Spirit*, 71.

the truth that injustice comes from the human heart and its will to do unjustly. "But resisters also recognize the evil existing in social structures and political systems, in the backbreaking work of some so that others might be idle; in unequal, disparate pay and benefits withheld; in unfair legal practices that allow the guilty to go free."[20] Resisters recognize evil in many places and in many forms. "For them, unless resistance to all of this exists in some form of spirituality, the ever threatening power of evil remains unacknowledged."[21] Harris writes:

> Resisters live their spirituality by speaking for the bruised child, or sheltering the battered woman. Rather than give people a meal of fish — although they do that — they teach people how to fish. They are themselves when working for better housing or better health care or better schooling for those who most need it. They are passionate about social issues, and in all honesty, some of us hate to see them coming because they so easily prick our consciences. They are people of whom their friends say, "She never seems to think of herself," or "She's a soft touch," when the truth of resisters' spirituality is that they are most themselves when confronting and changing the circumstances that damage lives. Such is their way of making the Mystery of God present in the world.[22]

Resisters are prophets who speak the truth and oppose the dominant culture. As prophets girls are called by God to "nurture, nourish, and evoke a consciousness and perception alternative to the consciousness and perception of the dominant culture."[23] Girls of color instinctively experience an alternative consciousness to the white middle-class dominant culture when they are subjected to racism and gender bias in

---

20. Ibid.
21. Ibid.
22. Ibid., 71–72.
23. Walter Brueggemann, *The Prophetic Imagination* (Philadelphia: Fortress Press, 1978), 13.

their classrooms. In my chapter "God and Grandmothers" Nicolé resists the subtle racial attacks from her teacher; yet she needs a means
of utilizing the potential of her resistance more widely, not only for
her benefit but also for other girls who might experience racism in
their classes. In Pat Davis's chapter, "Okay with Who I Am," Sandra, LaToya, and Keva all resist the many forms of homophobia they
experience and in doing so express an alternative consciousness and
a prophetic posture against racism and homophobia. As they become
more savvy, they will find ways to channel this instinctive resistance
toward transformation of the sins of racism and homophobia.

On the other hand there are girls who lack instinctive resistance
and fall victim to those who want to make then invisible, to those who
harass them sexually, and to the sexism, racism, and classism in their
families, schools, and churches.[24] In Laura Donaldson's chapter, "From
'Wanton Girle' to the Woman Who Fell from the Sky," Molley is a
victim of systems of economic oppression, poverty, and racism affecting
Native American people. She offers little or no form of resistance to
these assaults hurled at her. The working-class white girls in Dori
Baker's chapter, "Love Letters in a Second-Hand Hope Chest," are
victims of patriarchy and sexism, some only minimally resisting these
psychological attacks. These girls need to become aware of how they
are being oppressed and learn to resist it. By doing so, they will be
transformed into the prophets God is calling them to be and hence
will offer an alternative consciousness for transformation of patriarchy
and sexism. Resisters live out an opposing spirituality that is prophetic.

Practicing Resistance with Girls

Empowering adolescent girls to become resisters to oppression and
therefore to become prophets of God is the challenge of the practice
of resistance. Instinctive resistance needs to be refined to become a

---

24. Lyn Mikel Brown, *Raising Their Voices: The Politics of Girls' Anger* (Cambridge,
Mass.: Harvard University Press, 1998), 3. I have expanded Brown's review of the
literature on how girls are victimized to include issues of race and class.

prophetic way of being good to self and others. Girls who lack instinctive resistance need to develop this form of spirituality. From bell
hooks and Lyn Mikel Brown, two feminist scholars well versed in feminist practices of resistance with girls, I have gleaned a list of practices
that will help girls become prophetic resisters to race, class, gender,
and sexual orientation oppression.[25]

1. Girls of color should be encouraged to resist white supremacy
   as an epistemological standpoint, so that they come to know the
   world by always perceiving whiteness as a sign to be interrogated.

2. Girls of color and poor and working-class white girls should practice ways of protecting themselves from objectifying interaction.
   Girls should practice occasional segregation. Integration should
   not be seen as a demand or obligation.

3. Girls should be encouraged to "love the skin you're in." They
   should love blackness, brownness, slanted-eyes, round hips, big
   lips, and their heritages. They should decolonize their minds from
   believing that white is the norm and anything that is not white
   suggests inferiority, self-negation, and inadequateness.

4. Girls should affirm precociousness, outspokenness, subjectivity,
   and anger. Anger is the catalyst for movements that can transform the evils of the world. Our task is to help girls turn anger
   into knowledge.

5. Those who journey with girls should listen and look for their
   girls' resistance in all the subtle ways this might occur.

6. Creative refusal should be encouraged.

7. Alternative stories should be told in the face of victimization to racism, patriarchy, sexism, economic oppression, and
   homophobia.

---

25. Ibid. The practices I adopt from Lyn Mikel Brown are primarily found in her
chapter "Educating the Resistance," 198–224. bell hooks, *Killing Rage: Ending Racism*
(New York: Henry Holt Company), 108–18.

Resisting with Miriam

Miriam, the prophet and priest, is co-leader with Aaron and with Moses.[26] A mammoth conflict arises and Miriam, accompanied by Aaron, resists Moses' authority. In the wilderness, as they move from site to site, Miriam challenges Moses:

> Has the Lord spoken only through Moses?
> Has he not spoken through us also? (Num. 12:2)

Miriam admonishes Moses, teaching him that "all the Lord's people" includes women. As "the prophet" she has already spoken for God at the sea. So now amid the brambles and bushes that entangle them in the wilderness Miriam demands an equal sharing of the prophetic leadership.

> And the Lord hears it. (Num. 12:2)

Does the Lord punish Miriam for speaking out, for speaking up, for resisting the status quo?[27]

Resilience

The spiritual practices of realization and resistance among girls yield resilience. This is spiritual fortitude by which a girl's strength of mind empowers her to refocus, regather, reconnect, and recenter courageously amid dehumanizing adversity. A healthy spirituality for a girl includes the capacity to re-form the self when oppression de-forms her. Lynn Westfield, a womanist religious educator, describes resilience as "mastering the terrain of the oppressive context so well that one re-creates and heals the self in the very midst of chaos. It is mastering the

---

26. Trible, "Bring Miriam Out of the Shadows," 21.
27. Trible argues that the conflict between Miriam, Aaron, and Moses was due to priestly matters of leadership rather than Moses' Cushite wife. She questions other interpretations. While I acknowledge the interpretation of racial conflict, here I embrace the interpretation of struggle for priestly power.

ability to see one's self in a life-affirming light while the world around would shroud her in shadow."[28] Resilience is spiritual tenacity.[29] It is "about finding ways of living within one's context and understanding the context so well that one reconstitutes the self while in chaos (but not out of chaos) to see one's self in a positive light while the world around would say the opposite."[30] Girls exercise resilience when they reintegrate who they are amid the scattering forces of a racist, classist, sexist, and homophobic social landscape.

When I think of exemplars of this type of spirituality I am drawn to the life of Fannie Lou Hamer, a civil rights activist from Mississippi and a founder of the Mississippi Freedom Democratic Party (MFDP). Hamer showed a tenacity, determination, and perseverance few thought possible, given the powers of apartheid in the segregated South.[31] Her fortitude was grounded in a deep piety and Christian faith. She embodied courage, determination, and a capacity to recenter amid oppressive chaos. During the 1964 Democratic Convention, Hamer demonstrated extraordinary leadership regarding the seating of the MFDP delegation. The Democratic Party offered only two seats for the MFDP delegation instead of seating all the delegates. Hamer forced the hand of the male leadership of the MFDP; they rejected the compromise, and none of its delegates were seated. During that same convention Hamer stirred the hearts and minds of America to awareness of the realities of racial oppression in the South. In the crosshairs of the television camera, Hamer told her story of the egregious beating she, Annelle Ponder, and teenager June Johnson received in the Wionna, Mississippi, jail. These women had attempted to desegregate the waiting area of the bus station but were arrested and viciously beaten with leaded leather straps. Hamer was "permanently

---

28. N. Lynn Westfield, *Dear Sisters: A Womanist Practice of Hospitality* (Cleveland: Pilgrim Press, 2001), 8.

29. Ibid., 7.

30. Ibid.

31. Paula Giddings, *When and Where I Enter: The Impact of Black Women on Race and Sex in America* (New York: Bantam Books, 1985), 288.

debilitated by the assault and disfigured so badly that she wouldn't allow her family to see her for a month."[32]

This vicious event in Hamer's life illustrates her spiritual fortitude. It also shows us that "resilience connotes a more communal sense of being and belonging."[33] No doubt sixteen-year-old June Johnson experienced the communal nature of resilience. Euvester Simpson, a seventeen-year-old who shared the cell with Hamer, was also a member of this community of women. Although she was not physically beaten, she experienced the psychological trauma of hearing the cries and seeing the wounds of Hamer, Johnson, and Ponder. Euvester, and certainly June, came to know the communal nature of resilience as teenagers apprenticed to Hamer and Ponder. The combination of community and resilience among women and girls is characteristic of stories of the girls in this volume, suggesting the importance of relational practices of resilience.

Practicing Resilience with Girls

Nurturing resiliency in girls as an aspect of a healthy spirituality can be thought of as an apprenticeship. The process requires the presence of an experienced woman who accompanies a girl on the road to resilience. A mother, a grandmother, an aunt, or a "play mama" joins a girl on the journey. Hand in hand toward resilience a woman and a girl will discover "self-actualization, a growing together, a sense of ripeness, thriving, and experience of 'go!' "[34] They are both teachers and learners.

There are three ingredients for a girl-and-woman apprenticeship toward resilience. They are re-couraging, re-centering, and re-creating. These components are not invariant steps but concurrent practices among resilient girls and women that together signal a central characteristic of resilience, which is simultaneity. Spiritual fortitude requires

---

32. Ibid., 290.
33. Westfield, *Dear Sisters*, 7.
34. Ibid.

women and girls to practice courage, centering, and creating at the same time.

Re-couraging means returning, time and time again, to that state of mind where confidence confronts fear and self-assurance faces challenge. It is about fitting, over and over again, into one's audacious self. Hamer practiced re-couraging in jail, during protest marches against Jim Crow, during voter registration campaigns, and even in her home when attacked by the Ku Klux Klan. Girls also practice re-couraging in their schools, homes, and churches as they confront sexual harassment and abuse time and again.

Re-centering is praying back to the place of true identity. It is home in the Holy Spirit, the returning to the inner sanctum of God. Re-centering replenishes the soul in the Spirit of God continuously. Moments of silence, the whisper of a mantra, or the verse of a song are all aids to re-centering. It can happen while standing at the hub of conflict and confusion. Hamer re-centered when she tilted her head back and belted out verses of "This Little Light of Mine, I'm Gonna Let it Shine" during mass meetings, protest marches, and vigils. A girl can re-center, in silence or aloud, even as physical or verbal violence encroaches upon her. Praying one's self back to the center of true identity over and over again happens simultaneously with re-couraging.

Re-creating is regeneration of the mind, the crafting of new thoughts and new strategies. It is thinking on your feet. It is the recharging and renewal of the imagination in the moment. It can be conceived of as engineering a new approach, process, or mechanism when others fail to work sufficiently. In the ideal situation re-creation happens in solitude or among trusted others for self-reflection and meditation in a setting away from the maddening crowd. However, when things start to crumble and crash a girl needs the skill of re-creating on the spot, of thinking of a new strategy on her feet. Hamer constantly sharpened her ability to "think on her feet" as a member of the Student Nonviolent Coordinating Committee engaged in voter registration, education, and mobilization in Mississippi. A girl can also learn to "think on her feet" regardless of the challenging situation. Re-creating over and over again happens simultaneously with re-couraging and re-centering.

The practices of resilience beg the question of context. Where do women and girls hone the skills of resilience for lived experience? Among the many possible places are concealed gatherings where women and girls practice hospitality.[35] As reflected in the examples above, resilience happens in the very activities of justice work and sociopolitical activism. These examples are only two contexts in which women and girls can journey toward resilience.

Resilience with Miriam

The Lord punished Miriam severely for her priestly and prophetic protest against Moses. She becomes "leprous, as white as snow" (Num. 12:10). Aaron's cry to Moses on her behalf moves him to compassion and Moses cries to the Lord, "O God, please heal her!" (Num. 12:13). Yet the Lord is firm. Seven days must Miriam be shut out of the camp with skin as white as snow. For seven days Miriam sits and fights back the shame with fortitude. Miriam is a resilient prophet. "The people did not set out on the march until Miriam had been brought in again" (Num. 12:15).

Ritual

Wind Hughes writes: "With ceremonies and rituals we can make a moment or a day sacred, or honor something or someone important to us."[36] Ritual is a fitting essential for nurturing a healthy spirituality in adolescent girls. It is also an organic way of refueling the cycle of movements from realization, to resistance, and then resilience. "Rituals are a natural expression of acknowledging and experiencing

---

35. Ibid., 4. For Lynn Westfield hospitality is a foundational practice of resilience among African American women.

36. K. Wind Hughes and Linda Wolf, *Daughters of the Moon, Sisters of the Sun: Young Women and Mentors on the Transition to Womanhood* (Gabriola Island, B.C., Canada: New Society), 39.

something greater than ourselves."[37] Rituals complete our spirituality.[38] This is especially true for women and girls when they create the ritual, are included in the ceremony, and are placed in the position of the celebrant.[39]

Women have engaged in the practice of ritual-creating for centuries. During the last twenty-five years or more there has been a resurgence of rituals among women. These form three broad categories: (1) rituals that celebrate "the presence of Mystery is at the center of creation"; (2) rituals that celebrate Mother Earth nourishing human life paralleled with stories of the women who have nourished us; (3) and "rituals addressing critical times and crises known only to women, especially first menstruation."[40]

Wind Hughes describes ritual-creating as expressing what is in our own hearts and spirit. She continues: "When creating a ritual, I spend time contemplating the person, the holy day, or the season it will celebrate. I try to discover what it means to me. What do I want to honor, ask for, or pray for? We can speak about our appreciation, ask for guidance or healing, or design a ritual to raise our consciousness."[41] Hughes and a group of thirty-five women and girls built a Moon Lodge, a place to go for retreats and to hold celebrations, as well as a place to go when they were bleeding on their moon cycles. Each participant joined in decorating the Moon Lodge, creating a beautiful and functional place. The hearth/altar holds "incense, candles, photographs, postcards, feathers, stones, poems, and even a vial of someone's menstrual blood." There is a life-sized mannequin of a Crone, holding a staff that was once paraded through the forest during a ritual honoring and celebrating the wisdom of older women. There is a journal there for women and girls to write in, and small instruments and drums

---

37. Ibid.
38. Harris, *Dance of the Spirit*, 122.
39. Ibid.
40. Ibid.
41. Hughes and Wolf, *Daughters of the Moon*, 40.

for making music. Pillows and blankets abound in the Moon Lodge providing a warm and cozy environment. Hughes writes:

> Our lives have become so removed from experiences like these, and it is rare these days to have a community to share and celebrate with. I am grateful for the friends and community that have grown here on this island and for the sacred celebrations we have shared together. The time that I take for ritual is special to me and helps me to remain awake and deeply aware of life.[42]

These experiences of ritual-creating provide a template for rituals that nurture the spirituality of girls who are assaulted daily by racism, sexism, classism, and heterosexism.

Practicing Rituals with Girls

Rituals are necessary for nurturing a wholesome spirituality in girls. Rituals complete our spirituality. It would be ideal to create a place of ritual-making like the Moon Lodge, but for many of us, like the girls in this book, we are not afforded the resources to expend on building such a place. We can, however, create a sacred space where girls and women can create rituals for all the events of our lives, including celebrations as well as rituals for healing and mourning what we have lost. Rituals for girls on the margins of society must include these events and simultaneously affirm them for who they are and all that they can become. However, like the women and girls who engaged in ritual-creating in the Moon Lodge, girls from the margins of society can also create rituals with women on the journey with them, informal rituals as well as formal ones. Ritual-creating does not require a formula but can be informed by "spiritual practices"[43] that have been passed down to us through the centuries.

Dancing is an important way of honoring our spirit in rituals for girls and women. Dancing is also integral to the spiritual discipline of

---

42. Ibid., 41.
43. Dorothy Bass, ed., *Practicing Our Faith* (San Francisco: Jossey Bass, 1997).

honoring the body.[44] The body kinetically reveals the revitalization of a girl's spirit and the "aliveness" of the Holy Spirit within her. Dancing is essential for ritual-making for girls who are oppressed and the women who pledge to journey with them.

Dancing with Miriam

Miriam, the prophet, danced and sang unto Yahweh at the bank of the river for Israel's victory over Egypt. The women and perhaps all the people were moved to join her in this ritual.

> Then the prophet Miriam, Aaron's sister, took a tambourine in her hand; and all the women went out after her with tambourines and with dancing. And Miriam sang to them:
>
> > Sing to the LORD, for he has triumphed gloriously;
> > horse and rider he has thrown into the sea.
> > (Exod. 15:20–21)

Their hips swiveled and swayed and their hands waved in the air. Miriam the prophet, the sister of Aaron and Moses, danced and sang unto the Lord.

Conclusion

Nurturing the sacredness within girls on the margins of society is the challenge of women and men who value their sacredness. The stories of their lives reveal to us the contours of the challenge. When we faithfully journey with girls like those in this book as they seek to become their most sacred selves, we, too, like feathers in the wind, will dance through the gates of heaven and be at peace.

---

44. Stephanie Paulsell writes about the spiritual discipline of honoring the body in Bass, *Practicing Our Faith*. Although Paulsell does not specifically discuss dancing, it is clear from the conceptualization of honoring the body that dancing can be included.

CPSIA information can be obtained
at www.ICGtesting.com
Printed in the USA
LVHW080210190320
650546LV00015B/960